The Three Lives of

JOSEPH CONRAD

OLIVIA COOLIDGE

Houghton Mifflin Company Boston 1972

Other books by

OLIVIA COOLIDGE

Caesar's Gallic War

Come By Here

Cromwell's Head

Egyptian Adventures

Gandhi

George Bernard Shaw

Greek Myths

The King of Men

Legends of the North

Lives of Famous Romans

The Maid of Artemis

Makers of the Red Revolution

Marathon Looks on the Sea

Men of Athens

People in Palestine

Roman People

Tales of the Crusades

The Trojan War

Winston Churchill and the Story
   of Two World Wars

LIBRARY OF CONGRESS CATALOG CARD NUMBER 72-75603

ISBN 0-395-13890-6

PRINTED IN THE U.S.A.

FIRST PRINTING   C

CONTENTS

Introduction

The life of Conrad falls into three parts, each so different that it is amazing any one man should have lived them all. Indeed, the Polish experience of his boyhood was so dreadful that we may well wonder how many children could have survived without psychological damage which would have prevented them from coping with any life at all. Conrad's reaction, which took the form of plunging into an entirely different atmosphere, was probably the only solution for him. It is difficult, if not impossible, to think of him as a bureaucrat, reasonably adjusted to the daily routine which this implies.

His breakaway from Poland to lead a life of adventure shows qualities as extraordinary as his earlier powers of survival. It is clear, for instance, that his gradual adaptation to the human community came from life on shipboard, where the obvious need for working with others produced a fellowship which was demanding, but not very deep. Almost always unwilling to make two voyages on the same ship, he went through the world for many years giving to others his courage, endurance, and physical effort, but retaining affections and thought to himself. For long periods he neither had nor seemed to want friends. An incident which he recounts from the time when he was night watchman on the *Duke of Sutherland* in port in Sydney was typical of his detachment. "On one occasion I had an hour or so of most intellectual conversation with a person whom I could not see distinctly, a gentleman from England with a cultivated voice, I on deck and he on the quay sitting on the case of a piano (landed out of our hold that afternoon), and smoking a cigar which smelt very good. We touched, in our discourse, upon science, politics, natural history, and opera singers. Then, after remarking abruptly, 'You seem to be rather intelligent, my man,' he informed me pointedly that his name was Mr. Senior, and walked off — to his hotel, I suppose." He was not pursued by Conrad, though his opportunities of intelligent conversation at that time were rare. He did not want friends.

That Conrad made a success of such a life seems extraordinary, but that he made it in a foreign country where he had no connections and where he landed at the age of twenty speaking no more than a few words of the language, is little short of miraculous. His own account of his examination for third officer well demonstrates the difficulties which his foreign accent and appearance set in his way.

Eventually he began to write. Eventually he married, and started on a third life as different from the other two as they had been from one another. The miracle of his mastery of English is but another illustration of his extraordinary powers of concentration when he cared to use them. That he now needed friends may seem less miraculous; but his power of attracting them, his genuine devotion to them were as remarkable a change from his earlier attitude as his love of his wife and family, or even his general dislike of foreign travel.

The character which ran through all these changes was highly gifted, forcible, and complex. His friends remarked that he was intensely alive and took the lead in company, not because he was not an excellent listener, but because his personality was unusually vivid. This is not to say that he was an easy man. If he had been, he must surely have failed somewhere and vanished unknown before he came to greatness. Struggling, as he constantly did with ill health and frayed nerves, he had a sudden quality about him which may be illustrated by the trivial occasion when he came out to greet callers and was stung by a wasp. "Leaping violently in the air and shouting, Damn! Blast! Bring an onion — bring a blue bag! he disappeared rapidly into the house." Such occasions were constantly arising in the Conrad household, triggered as often by irritation of nerves as some small accident.

Difficult he must have been, especially as he was subject, particularly during his writing life, to fits of depression, which were increased by his constant need to grind out work in order to earn money. It is remarkable, considering this pressure, how little bad work he wrote; but the qualities which made him a careful sailor made him incapable of producing second-rate writing while he could do better. Nevertheless, he was not all strength. His weaknesses included a tendency to give up and let go in moments of weariness, and this in later days was increased by the recurrence of gout.

These qualities did not prevent perhaps the most extraordinary of his achievements. He became known and loved by a wide circle of people in a country not his own, possessing a language which he never spoke like a native. Foreign in appearance, in manner, in temperament, he made himself a home in England, that most insular of nations, leaving, when he went, an empty place which has not been filled.

We are grateful to Culver Pictures, Inc.,
for permission to include photographs found on
pages ii, 132, 152, and 220; to The Bettmann
Archive, Inc., for photographs on pages 85 and 180;
to J. M. Dent and Son, Ltd., for photographs on
pages 9 and 25; and to the New York Public Library,
Picture Collection, for photographs on pages 37,
129, 172, 197, and 203.

FIRST LIFE

The Polish Prisoner

1

Death in Cracow

In 1795, Poland was forcibly divided among Russia, Prussia, and Austria, so that throughout the whole of the nineteenth century it did not exist as an independent nation. In 1869 the city of Cracow, now in Austrian Poland, was a town of about sixty thousand with a hundred churches and more splendid historical traditions than Warsaw itself. Well-placed for trade and in a mining area, it should have prospered; but like any city which has been wrenched from the lands with which it has historical connections, Cracow was barely holding its own, unimportant to Austria, and with its ancient lines of trade interrupted by Russian frontiers. To be sure, there was bustle in the great market square, where heavy cart horses clattered over irregular stones and street vendors gave their traditional yells; but in the side streets Cracow was very quiet. Out of one of these, about eight every morning in the early months of that year, emerged a frail dark boy of eleven with a schoolboy's satchel on his back, starting on his way through the great square toward the medieval Florian Gate, whose archway still marked the ancient walls. Three doors down from that gate on the second floor of one of the old houses was a small preparatory school. The boy went in, and presumably other boys did also, some of whom cheerfully made friends or started games. Perhaps this boy joined in the laughter, or perhaps he shrank into corners; but whatever he did was perfectly mechanical so that in afterlife he could not remember it.

What he did remember was the walk home through the ill-lit streets and the entry into a high-ceilinged drawing room which had seen better days and in which his father's possessions lay about half unpacked. Probably no one watched him come in and light the pair of candles which cast irregular shadows into the corners of the room while he did his homework. At some time or other the housekeeper of a canon of St. Mary's Cathedral, who lived upstairs, came down to get him a meal. She was a stout woman in a black dress with a cross hanging on her bosom, elderly, silent, and unused to children. She did what she came for and went away without saying much. The boy sat at a table, inking his fingers, as every child did in the days before ball-point pens, occasionally glancing at a tall white door across the room, which was kept closed. Now and then it would open just wide enough to let a nursing nun in her white coif come out and cross the room, perhaps to fetch something or to exchange duty with another sister. The nuns spoke seldom and in tones not much above a whisper. Sometimes, however, when the boy had finished his schoolwork, they saw him immersed in one of the books that lay around on tables, chairs, or even on the floor. Then the older nun would put a gentle hand on his head and expostulate in her usual murmur, "Perhaps it is not very good for you to read these books." In answer the boy merely looked up at her until, baffled by the expression in his eyes, she moved away.

Later on, on most evenings, the door would be opened a little wider for the boy to go in and say good night to his father, who often could do no more than lift his eyes in response. The boy would put his lips to the hand which lay on the coverlet and tiptoe out. Then he went off to bed in a room at the end of a corridor, where he cried himself to sleep without disturbing anyone.

"I don't know what would have become of me," he said of this period, "if I had not been a reading boy." The books that troubled the old nun were tales of Victor Hugo, rousing stories of adventures, or accounts of exploration. For an hour or two and over the endless holidays, the boy could escape to a world where people did things which were courageous, physical, direct, and which had no bearing on a revolt doomed from before its start, a Russian prison, or death moving closer with steps as inevitable as the muffled footfalls of the nursing nuns. Already at nine he had had a passion for polar exploration and for the perilous journeys of Mungo Park in the western Sudan, of Bruce in Abyssinia, of Burton and Speke in Tanganyika. In his first school atlas, published in 1852, the center of Africa was a white, unexplored blank. Carefully he traced in the now-discovered outline of Lake Tanganyika; and once in the early days of school — for he had till recently been tutored by his father —

he exposed himself to the laughter of the group by putting his finger on a blank space in Africa which represented, though no one knew it at the time, the upper Congo and saying, "Some day I'm going *there!*" He might as well have said, "Some day I'm going to get out of this town where every holiday is a day of public mourning for past grandeurs. I am going to get out of dead Poland into a world where men can do simple, positive things."

Apollo Korzeniowski took such a long time dying that his son had no tears left for his funeral. Cracow was not unaware of a man who, though an utter failure, had sacrificed his life for his country. A long procession wound its way out of the Florian Gate toward the cemetery, first the hearse drawn by black horses, then the small boy walking alone, then the clergy in their surplices, schoolchildren in procession, dignitaries of the University, delegations of the trade guilds. The town turned out to see Apollo go to his grave, and his name was added to a long list of Polish patriot martyrs. A few years later when the boy was fourteen, the city council made him a freeman of Cracow, exempt from taxes for life. Unfortunately, they could not make him an Austrian instead of a Russian subject.

This miserable, if honored, death in Cracow was no more than a reflection of what had been going on in Poland since its loss of independence seventy-five years earlier. The history of two families which combined to produce a great English novelist affords examples which could be duplicated a thousand times. The partition of Poland had coincided more or less with the French Revolution. Indeed, one of the reasons why this revolution grew too strong to suppress was

that the powerful countries of eastern and central Europe
were too deeply involved in rivalry over Poland to interfere
in France. Not unnaturally, when Napoleon embarked on
his career of European conquest, Poles rallied to his support,
while he let it be known that he intended to restore the land
to its ancient independence. The truth of the matter was that
Napoleon had not much interest in Poland, save as a convenient recruiting ground. To conquer Austria and Prussia,
he needed to appease the Russians. To conquer Russia, he
needed the cooperation and the good will, as far as he could
get it, of Austria and Prussia. There was no moment at
which he felt it wise to offend all three. However, he encouraged the Poles and, within the limits of imperial policy,
showed favor to them. The consequence was that an all-
Polish army, actually commanded by Polish generals, fought
with Napoleon through most of his European campaigns.
In 1808, this was joined by Nicholas Bobrowski, sixteen years
old and the younger son of a well-to-do Polish landowner.
By 1813, Bobrowski had fought all over Europe and attained
the rank of lieutenant, together with two distinguished deco-
rations, Knight of the Legion of Honor, and the Polish Cross
for Valor. In 1812, he had been part of the immense expedition which Napoleon assembled for the invasion of Russia
and had been through the horrors of its winter retreat from
Moscow, from which only a few thousands returned alive.

At one point in that retreat, he and two fellow officers
lost the whole army in a blizzard and found themselves in
the Lithuanian forest after wandering off their course for
three days. Nicholas Bobrowski's history would have ended
there had they not had the good fortune, while approaching

a fenced village in which they knew some Cossacks had been quartered, to be attacked by a dog which not only barked at them, but found a gap in the fence and came rushing out. A cavalry sword dispatched it; and at a safe distance in the forest, the fugitives were able to kindle a fire on the snow. The dog was unattractive food, being unhealthily fat and disgustingly mangy; but starving men were in no position to be nice. Nicholas Bobrowski rejoined the army and was in good enough condition to fight for Napoleon at the Battle of Leipzig in 1813, soon after which the Emperor was forced into exile in Elba.

Nicholas Bobrowski went home to the Polish Ukraine, now part of Russia. It stood to reason that, as Russia, Prussia, and Austria were on the victorious side, no freedom could be expected for Poland in the new Europe. Alexander I, the Russian Emperor, however, was inclined to let bygones be bygones as far as individuals were concerned. When Napoleon escaped from Elba and began the famous hundred days which culminated in his final defeat at Waterloo, Bobrowski did not join him. When asked by friends about the matter, he merely muttered, "No money. No horse. Too far to walk."

The arrangement made in the peace of 1815 was that the Kingdom of Poland should be reconstituted in the part of Poland which belonged to Russia, but that its King should be the Russian Tsar. Alexander appointed his next brother Constantine first as general of the Polish army and later as his governor in Poland. Constantine fell in love with and married a Polish lady, renouncing his right of succession in order to do so. For about fifteen years, therefore, Poland actually existed as an entity of its own inside Russia with its own army, in which Bobrowski was a captain, and having its laws, its language, and its traditional Parliament. This was an arrangement, however, which could not last. The Tsar, whose rule was absolute in Russia, was offended by the activities of the Polish assembly. Protected though they were by Constantine, the Poles did not love him; and few historians have anything favorable to say about him. In 1825, when Alexander died, he was succeeded by his youngest brother Nicholas, far abler but also more autocratic. A Polish rebellion broke out five years later, which Constantine by inept handling allowed to become formidable. Pretty soon the whole Polish army, polished to a professional pitch by Constantine's own love of drilling, joined in the revolt against the Russians.

At the outbreak of this struggle, Captain Nicholas Bobrowski had been in charge of procuring cavalry remounts in Russia, since the Poles did not raise their own horses. Hastily arrested with his entire detachment, he was interned in a remote Russian province, at personal liberty, but forced to report to the military commandant daily. Long before he was allowed to return home, the rebellion had been crushed, the constitution of Poland dissolved, and measures of Russification put in hand. Soon Polish was no longer officially used in the law courts; Polish universities were dissolved, and students transferred to St. Petersburg or Kiev. School instruction was in Russian. Captain Bobrowski was offered rank in the Russian army, but he found no place in it for his

Napoleonic medals or his devotion to the ideals of Polish freedom. Retired on half-pension, he returned home to his brother.

Nicholas had been a younger son, so that it was natural for him to choose an army career. Joseph Bobrowski had remained on his estate of Novofastov in the Ukraine because he was needed there, both by his family and by Poland. He was a sound provincial gentleman, well educated but not bookish, a good estate manager and a sport lover with a famous stable of steppe horses. In person he was bald and thin with a hooked nose; in temperament he was agreeable and quick-witted, but invincibly obstinate. Devoted to his six sons and two daughters, he had brought them up very much as a family unit. In particular, he had imbued his sons with a feeling of protectiveness toward their sisters. The elder, Evelina, was according to the family very handsome, though her surviving portrait does not suggest this. She was certainly talented, gifted at languages, temperamental, and with a brilliance which made her conspicuous. Her younger sister Teofila was quite outshone in looks and talent, but possessed an affectionate nature which made her brothers prize her even more highly. Such treasures needed careful disposition, and it was a great grief to Joseph Bobrowski when his high-strung Evelina fell in love at sixteen with a friend of her elder brother Thaddeus.

Apollonius, or Apollo, Korzeniowski was a young man with a social background similar to Evelina's. His father, Theodor, had also fought under Napoleon, had been twice wounded, and had gained the Polish Medal for Valor. He had taken part in the 1830 uprising and had the name of a breezy fellow with a very good opinion of himself backed by little common sense. After losing most of his inherited property through speculation, he had been forced to retire to his wife's estate, where he earned a living administering the far larger possessions of a neighbor on the vast rolling plains of the Ukraine, where fifteen hundred acres was considered a small estate and where wealthy homes contained three

Evelina Korzeniowska, Joseph Conrad's mother

hundred servants. Surprisingly, perhaps, Korzeniowski spent some of his time in literary pursuits, producing a five-act tragedy so dull that according to his grandson nobody had ever managed to read it through. Intellectually, he was a liberal of an impractical sort and, though engaged for his living in managing an estate where serfs were sold like cattle, allowed himself opinions that such things ought not to be. Of his three sons, the eldest, Robert, inherited the gambling and drinking strain; the youngest, Hilary, the social ideals and the taste for estate management. The middle son, Apollo, improved considerably on his father's literary talents.

Apollo Korzeniowski had been born in 1820, an unfortunate time for a Pole, since it exposed him while growing up to Russian bitterness after 1830 as well as to the repressive measures of Tsar Nicholas I, who was converting Russia and Poland alike into a police state. When, for instance, Apollo applied for a passport in order to study in Berlin, France, or Italy, it was refused as part of a general ban on foreign travel, which Nicholas felt was unsettling to young men. There being no Polish university extant, Apollo went to St. Petersburg, where he devoted himself to oriental studies, a safe, nonpolitical subject. Presently, however, he changed to French literature, which was more controversial, since it was then concerned with romantic ideas about national or personal freedom. It is questionable whether Nicholas I achieved a great deal by forcing Polish students to take their education in St. Petersburg. To be sure, they learned Russian; but they formed their own groups, talked Polish politics, and read Polish literature, which was undergoing a period of romantic renaissance.

Most of these young Poles had little to look forward to. Nicholas hoped to attract many into the Russian bureaucracy, but Polish recruits to public service existed to do their best for Polish connections and were corrupt or careless in their dealings with Russians. Such a career was revolting to idealistic, impractical men like Apollo Korzeniowski. At the same time he had no secure inheritance, no family estate to support him. With his literary tastes, he might have made a good professor in a Polish university, had one existed. As things were, he stayed six years in St. Petersburg and left without bothering to take his degree. He ran up a fair number of debts, wrote Polish poems, and had a good deal of success in literary salons. He later followed this up by producing a play called *Because of the Money,* which won a prize in Warsaw, and *A Comedy,* a five-act play in verse satirizing modern manners.

Since he could not afford to stay indefinitely in St. Petersburg, Apollo retired to his father's estate, where he nominally helped with management, but read or wrote a good deal and visited extensively, seeking to find exceptions to the limited outlook which was characteristic of Polish provincial society. Ugly but intelligent, sarcastic but never malicious, emotional and idealistic, Apollo was easily able to make himself liked, especially by those who had more ability than their country neighbors. Among such friends, Thaddeus Bobrowski, nine years younger than Apollo, was starting his studies at St. Petersburg, with the intention of following a legal career. A highly practical young man, whose balance and sanity helped make up for the difference in their ages, Thaddeus found himself at a loss to understand Korzeniowski but thought him the only man in the district he really could talk to.

The connection having been made, it was natural that Apollo should visit the Bobrowskis. Mme Bobrowska, Evelina's mother, certainly liked him; and if Bobrowski had objections to him as a friend for Thaddeus, he was wise enough to trust in his son's good sense. As a husband for Evelina, their precious jewel, he was not to be considered for a moment. Twenty-eight years old when he fell in love with Evelina, Apollo had no purpose or profession. This might have been overcome, for the young man had connections, while the Bobrowskis also had some influence. It was not so much Apollo's circumstances that Joseph Bobrowski disliked for his daughter as his character and that of the Korzeniowskis in general. There was evidently an impractical strain in the family. The father, to put it bluntly, was an outright failure; and neither of the brothers showed much promise. Apollo himself was not reliable; he talked well but wildly on subjects about which imprudent views were dangerous.

Polish patriotism had not in these difficult years shown signs of flagging; it had rather risen to new heights and in the opinion of practical men men like Joseph Bobrowski was going a little mad. Before 1830, when patriotic literature if prudently disguised could at least be published, the Polish poet Mickiewitz had written an epic called *Konrad Wallenrod,* set in medieval times to placate the Russians. The hero of this poem, a young Lithuanian Pole, had been captured in boyhood by the Teutonic Knights, who were a German military order crusading against the Lithuanian pagans.

Konrad adopted Christianity, became one of the Knights,
and eventually rose to be their leader. Now at last in a position to avenge the slaughter of his people, he deliberately led
the Knights into a trap in which they perished. *Konrad
Wallenrod* was understood by every Pole to mean that temporary service to the conquerer might be permissible, alle-
giance never. This, though in a passive way, was the position
of men like Bobrowski, keeping alive Polish traditions while
awaiting some international change which might restore
their lost independence. Napoleon had seemed to offer a
chance, but this had faded. Like Konrad Wallenrod, Joseph
Bobrowski was prepared to wait a long time.

After the rebellion of 1830, which might possibly have
succeeded if it had attracted international support, the poet
Mickiewitz went into exile and became a professor of Polish
literature in Paris. He was followed by many of the most
enterprising of the Polish aristocracy and gentry, who saw no
future for themselves in their country under existing conditions. Divorced by exile from reality, the passion and despair
of Mickiewitz and those who worshiped him became un-
bounded. In another long work the poet depicted a hero
who sacrificed personal loves and desires in order to become
a pure patriot. "Let Konrad [Wallenrod] be my name from
now," he carved on the stone of his dungeon, "instead of
Augustus." Going to further extremes, Mickiewitz proclaimed that martyred Poland was a mystic incarnation of
crucified Christ and was destined to redeem nations by her
suffering as Christ had redeemed individuals. This led to
even more curious parallels. Christ, as the Apostle's Creed
puts it, "was dead and buried. He descended into Hell. The

third day He rose again from the dead." To Mickiewitz, the partition of Poland was its crucifixion and 1830 its descent into Hell. On a third occasion still to come, God would raise Poland triumphant, leader of a new age and spiritual savior of Europe.

Such high-flown mysticism was so unreasonable that it was bound to offend Poles who, vanquished in 1830 when Poland at least had an army, were now enduring the realities of Russian oppression. The suggestion, implied if not explicitly stated, that Poland would have God on her side and would therefore need no weapons for her final resurrection was in flat contradiction to the experience of older men. Joseph Bobrowski may well have felt distrustful of the effect of someone like Korzeniowski on his sons. He must certainly have been horrified at the thought of entrusting his daughter to a man whose enthusiasms might outstrip his common sense. Evelina, educated at home by governesses, chaperoned and shielded, had been brought up to confound patriotism with religion. It had never occurred to Bobrowski that any female would need to advise or restrain her husband's ardor. A woman's business was to implant patriotic fervor in her sons.

Bobrowski flatly refused consent to the match; and his wife, despite her personal liking for Apollo, was easily brought to admit he was unreliable. Evelina submitted to her father's judgment, but could not do so without an inner struggle. Emotional and shielded by her menfolk from contact with practical affairs, she could not control her love for Korzeniowski. The strain produced hysterical scenes and symptoms of illness which may have amounted to a nervous breakdown.

For three years this situation continued, while Bobrowski hoped that time would heal his daughter's wound. Before this occurred, however, he himself was stricken by a stroke or heart attack and died at a moment when none of the family was at home but Evelina.

Thaddeus, now at St. Petersburg studying law, was at this time the oldest son, since his brother Stanislas, an officer in the Guards and beloved by all who knew him, had recently died. He threw up his profession and came home to manage the family affairs. The widowed Mme Bobrowska, who was not well, moved temporarily with her daughters to the house of a friend who lived nearer to a doctor. The other boys being at schools or colleges, Thaddeus was left alone, except that his sisters took turns in driving over to cheer up his spirits. One winter day, Teofila started out on this errand in threatening weather, accompanied by a groom and a coachman. Snow started and soon worsened until several miles from their destination they lost the road altogether and stuck in a snowdrift. The men were trying to dig out, but Teofila was sure the road was not far back and that they ought to walk. They soon discovered the route, but snow was falling so thickly that it was four hours before they struggled home. The servants did their utmost for their young mistress; but she arrived wet and chilled to the bone, developed pneumonia, and was dead in a few weeks.

This third tragedy, occurring not long after the other two, had a serious effect on Evelina, who was already emotionally upset. Devotedly she assured her family that she would not marry a man of whom her dear dead father had disapproved. Her health, less strong than her will, failed to an alarming degree until, it seems probable, tuberculosis threatened. After several more years of struggle, Mme Bobrowska came gradually around to the view that Evelina's life depended on the marriage. Thaddeus, now head of the family, could not resist such an argument. Negotiations took time, for Evelina herself had to be persuaded, while Korzeniowski, despairing of his suit, had moved to Podolia, a distant part of Russian Poland, where he was managing the estate of a connection. In circles such as these, every gentleman was supposed to know how to run an estate, while there were often widowed relatives who needed help. At least, therefore, Korzeniowski was earning an income. Though the Bobrowskis were not especially wealthy, Evelina would have a respectable dowry, which ought to enable the married pair to manage. Thus in 1856, about eight years after their first meeting, Apollo and Evelina were finally married. The bridegroom was thirty-six years old and the bride not quite twenty-four.

2

A Tragic Childhood

Unquestionably the Korzeniowski marriage was happy if mutual devotion can of itself bring happiness. At first all was honeymoon weather. Mme Bobrowska lent money to help the young pair lease an estate which should, with proper management, support them. Here, near Berdichev in the Ukraine, a son was born to them in December 1857, and christened Józef Teodor Konrad Nałęcz Korzeniowski.

It is necessary for us to make sense of this name because, peculiar though it may appear to English-speaking readers, it was going to become famous in English literature. We may therefore note that Józef and Teodor were simply the names of his two grandparents. Nałęcz was a piece of his surname, distinguishing these Korzeniowskis from a different branch, which produced, incidentally, a well-known Polish novelist. Konrad was the essential name by which his parents called him. It came straight out of Mickiewitz, not from Konrad Wallenrod, but that purer patriot once named Augustus. Nothing could have indicated more clearly the political feelings of his parents, who were soon involved in a romantic bid for Poland's freedom. It was by this name, anglicized to Conrad, that the child was to be known for most of his life.

Unfortunately, a bachelor of thirty-six, a mystic and a poet, who had been a frequenter of literary salons and had in common with his father a hopeful way of hatching impractical schemes, was not easy to turn into an agriculturalist, merely because he had been born into the landowning class. Apollo made friends, even admirers among his neighbors, but writing and reading were more important to him than attending to business. Three years after the marriage, Evelina's dowry and Mme Bobrowska's money were more or less exhausted, so that Korzeniowski had to turn elsewhere for support.

He took his wife and child to Zhitomir, a lively provincial center, where he joined a group planning to publish popular literature for the education of peasants. It seems unlikely that this was profitable, but he also started in collaboration with a friend a translation into Polish of Victor Hugo's complete works and succeeded in getting a production for *Because of the Money*. Such activities, far more natural to him than farming, might very possibly have established him as a minor literary figure. Unfortunately, in the existing state of Poland, they were inseparable from political action.

The iron rule of Tsar Nicholas I had been broken by the disaster of the Crimean War. Shortly before the marriage of Apollo and Evelina, the Tsar had died a disappointed man, leaving his empire to Alexander II, a well-meaning, liberal monarch who perceived that the time had come to make concessions which would relieve the pressures on his discontented subjects. Accordingly, prisoners were released; and political exiles came flocking back into Poland. A Polish school of medicine was founded in Warsaw with the expectation of a national university to follow. These and similar concessions, far from reconciling Poles to their lot, merely gave opportunities to men who in no circumstances intended to put up with Russian rule. In fact, Poles themselves, more deeply divided than ever on the question of how to re-establish their country, began to split into "Reds," disciples of Mickiewitz, who wanted a revolt, however wild and impractical, and "Whites," among whom was Thaddeus Bobrowski, still insisting that until the international climate was fair, the cause was hopeless.

The intellectuals of Zhitomir were "Red," and indeed there is an obvious connection between educating peasants and starting a mass movement of revolt. About this time Apollo took to wearing the peasant costume of belted smock and knee boots which made him conspicuous in upper-class circles and no doubt attracted the attention of the police.

Meanwhile in Warsaw, the emotional and cultural center of the country, mass demonstrations against Russian rule were taking place, culminating in a violent clash in which a few people were killed. Apollo Korzeniowski was said by the Russians to have organized a requiem mass for these martyrs in Zhitomir, at which time Evelina publicly pinned on mourning cockades. This event took place early in 1861, and a month or two later Apollo joined the crowd of hot-headed patriots flocking to Warsaw. His excuse was the editorship of a new literary monthly, but the magazine provided little more than a meeting place for malcontents. Easily recognizable in his peasant costume, Apollo was one of the organizers of a further demonstration and, it is supposed, the author of a leaflet which called on the people to turn out for that occasion.

It is obvious that such activities were dangerous and Apollo had soon made himself a marked man. At first he had left his wife in Zhitomir, but her desire to join him and take a part in the work was as ardent as his. In the middle of 1861, she came to Warsaw with Conrad, who later remembered his mother admitting mysterious men to their apartment, noting that she was clad in the black of national mourning "worn in defiance of ferocious police regulations." Conrad was only three and a half, and his memory of dates was always imperfect. National mourning was not at this time forbidden, but it certainly was a conspicuous costume which hardly argued that Apollo or his wife were of a temperament to make successful conspirators. It is fair to say that private people depending on the masses to strengthen a revolt must make themselves conspicuous in some fashion, and it is hardly Korzeniowski's fault that he had neither the genius of Trotsky nor the underground abilities of Lenin. Nevertheless, there is no doubt that the Korzeniowskis were amateurish. For instance, before Evelina arrived from Zhitomir, she wrote her husband, commenting freely on what he was doing. Either the police were already opening his letters, or else he affectionately preserved them. In any case, they later formed part of the indictment against him.

By October 1861, patriots headed by a secret committee which Apollo had organized had staged a massive boycott of the municipal elections. The government of Warsaw was breaking down, and martial law was soon proclaimed. Apollo's reply on October 17 was to organize a secret central committee which controlled anti-Russian agitation until the outbreak of revolt. Four days later, he was arrested and imprisoned in the Warsaw citadel. Conrad, still not four years old, retained a confused memory of standing with his mother in the prison yard and seeing his father peering out through a barred window.

The investigation of Apollo's activities took about six months, not apparently because his treason was difficult to establish, but chiefly because in Russia things moved slowly. The verdict of the court was exile under prison conditions to somewhere in the Russian north. Evelina, who was determined to accompany her husband, may or may not have been accused and sentenced with him. According to one of Korzeniowski's friends, she was not; but she had to submit to the same conditions in order to go with him. Mme Bobrowska certainly came up from the Ukraine at some point in the proceedings to take charge of her little grandson. A photograph of the boy, dated July 1863, was found in the family archives inscribed in a childish hand, "To my dear Granny, who helped me send cakes to my poor Daddy in prison — grandson, Pole, Catholic, gentleman. Konrad." His parents might have been reduced to Russian convicts with numbers substituted for their names, but they rose above these facts in the pretensions which they transmitted to their son.

One of the reasons why the police were in no hurry to gather their information may well have been that the arrest took place in October. Traveling conditions in Russia were so incredibly bad that there could be no question of sending prisoners to the far north until winter eased, snow melted, and muddied roads dried out in early summer. Bobrowski and Korzeniowski connections had plenty of time to exercise what influence they possessed in hopes of getting the prisoners sent to a place which was not too desolate. Stanislas Bobrowski, Evelina's oldest brother, was still affectionately remembered by influential friends. Though not in themselves important, the two families could appeal to princely Polish aristocrats, connected by marriage with the Russian elite. Decisions in such cases as Apollo's were often influenced by a word in the right ear. It so happened that Korzeniowski had an old friend from St. Petersburg days who was governor of Perm; and he was allowed to petition to be sent to this place, whither he was actually dispatched in May 1862, in an official carriage built for security rather than comfort or speed, accompanied by his wife and son and two guards. The governor of Perm, however, who apparently had not been notified until the last minute of his arrival, perceived the awkwardness of treating an old friend as a convict, while at the same time he feared the effect on his own career of any kindness which might be reported. He declined the responsibility; and someone across whose desk Apollo's papers came wrote in an order for his transfer to Vologda. It was a slow death sentence for Evelina and eventually for her husband also.

Their journey, thus prolonged by the change of direction,

was one of terrible discomfort as they jolted daily along the endless untended Russian roads. By the time that they arrived near Moscow, little Conrad was dangerously ill; and his mother implored the guards to stop while a doctor was summoned. They were unwilling, but a bystander took the family's part and volunteered to take a message to a doctor at the university, whose name Apollo remembered. The doctor arrived, but while he administered medicine, the horses were being harnessed to the carriage. Apollo protested once more, supported by the doctor, who insisted the child would probably die if they went on. The guards, whose brutality was due to a fear of transgressing their orders, consented to wait while they consulted the local police. Back came the reply that the difficulty had been noted, but that the journey was to proceed because children were born only to die some time or another.

Little Conrad, who must at that time have had a tough constitution, survived this experience. Presently, however, Evelina became ill and grew so weak that she had to be carried in and out of the posting houses where they stayed the night. Luckily a passing officer, indignant at such treatment, reported to the local chief of police the escort's behavior. This time, the police chief rode out himself to investigate and discovered that Evelina was the sister of that Stanislas Bobrowski whose charm no one ever seemed to have forgotten. He stopped the journey and took her to a comfortable house in town till she recovered.

Vologda proved to be a small way station on the road to Archangel, one of Russia's few outlets to the sea and consequently a busy port in the short season when it was not frozen over. Near the edge of the Arctic Circle, Vologda was lashed in winter by cold winds off the White Sea, staying continuously at temperatures twenty-four to thirty degrees below zero. When the Korzeniowskis arrived, it was early summer, but the place was desolate in the extreme. "Vologda," Apollo wrote to one of his cousins, "is a great . . . marsh on which logs and trees are placed parallel to one another in crooked lines, everything rotting and shifting under one's feet; this is the only means of communication available to the natives . . . The climate consists of two seasons of the year: a white winter and a green winter. The white winter lasts nine-and-a-half months and the green one two-and-a-half. We are now at the onset of the green winter. It has already been raining ceaselessly for twenty-one days, and that's how it will be to the end."

Houses were wooden structures built on piles above the marsh, and in one of these the Korzeniowskis were quartered. Russian political prisoners under the Tsars were not, unless condemned to hard labor, sent to concentration camps. It was neglect rather than brutality which killed them. They were simply assigned quarters in some peasant's hut, given a bare subsistence allowance, and compelled to report at the police station every day in all weathers. If they were too ill to do so, the police chief had to be summoned to see for himself that they were still present. They were permitted to receive money and parcels from their friends and could occupy themselves as they chose. Trotsky, forty years later, wrote articles from Siberia. Lenin produced a book. But even had Apollo brought with him all the supplies he might need for such work, it could not have helped keep him or

Apollo Korzeniowski, Joseph Conrad's father

his family alive. To live in Vologda required not only special clothing but special skills. The Bobrowskis could and did send money, but the problem was by no means only financial. There were already twenty-one Polish exiles in the place, many of whom were suffering from scurvy. There was little fresh food to be had and, lacking land or knowledge of what could be gathered locally, the Poles went without. The prisoners made things worse by keeping themselves to themselves, too proud to speak Russian or to admit that they understood it unless they were forced to. Little Conrad, with a remarkable gift for languages, spent five years of his life in Russian exile, yet never admitted afterward that he knew more than a few words of the language. Most of the Polish exiles were priests, because one of the deepest divisions between Poland and Russia was that between the Catholic and Orthodox faiths. The Catholic clergy were in the forefront of the national movement, so that many of them had already been deported. The consequence was that there were few women and no children whatever except Conrad among the exiles.

Letters from Vologda made their slow way back to the Polish Ukraine, telling this dismal tale and asking for supplies of one sort or another. While they did so, the revolt that Apollo had helped to inspire broke out in an ill-organized uprising which was quenched in streams of blood without ever achieving any place in Russian history more important than a temporary nuisance. With it were swept away Robert Korzeniowski, his brother Hilary, and Stefan Bobrowski. Those who remained of the Bobrowski family renewed their efforts on behalf of their sister, whose health had steadily failed during the white winter of Vologda. Luckily the governor of Vologda was a compassionate man, happy to endorse a recommendation that the Korzeniowskis be transferred to a milder climate. Accordingly, in the summer of 1863, they were permitted to travel by themselves on parole to Chernigov, northeast of Kiev, where they were received with kindness by Prince Golitsin, the governor of

that place, who allowed Evelina three months' leave to visit
her family at Novofastov, taking young Conrad with her.

This occasion caused much joy but many tears to the
Bobrowskis. Evelina was seriously ill with tuberculosis, and
it was evident that she could not survive a northern climate,
even though somewhat milder than that of Vologda. In
other words, when she returned to her exile, her family must
say goodbye to her for ever. To six-year-old Conrad, un-
suspicious of this problem, Novofastov in the Ukraine appeared like heaven. Uncle Thaddeus was a widower with an
only daughter just Conrad's age. Josefina was a little princess
in his eyes with a couple of devoted nurses and a French
governess who was acute enough to perceive how the little
boy hungered for play and taught him to chatter in French
without his ever knowing he was doing lessons. All the
servants on the place were friendly and devoted. There was
a coachman who allowed him to hold the reins while the
horses were standing and to play with the big whip. There
was all he wanted to eat, and everyone was happy — or at
least he thought they were. People came and went all the
time, bringing with them excitement. Novofastov was the
happiest spot he could remember, and his mother called it
"home." Conrad never really remembered a home before
the disaster, so that Novofastov took that place in his affections.

His luck was running out, however. Some of the people
who came to visit were evidently doctors. About a month
before her leave was up, Evelina was so gravely ill that her
brothers petitioned the local governor for an extension of a
couple of weeks until she was able to travel. A short while

later, the police chief of the district drove quietly up to the
house at dusk and asked to see the master. "There," he said,
putting a paper into Thaddeus Bobrowski's hands, "pray
read this. I have no business to show this paper to you. It is
wrong of me. But I can't eat or sleep with such a job hanging over me."

Thaddeus Bobrowski looked at the document, which was
an order to disregard all explanations and excuses if Evelina
did not set out on the appointed day. She was forthwith to
be arrested and dispatched under escort to the prison hospital
at Kiev.

"For God's sake," the policeman said, absolutely wringing
his hands, "see that your sister goes away punctually on that
day. Don't give me this work to do with a woman — and
with one of your family, too. I simply cannot bear to think
of it."

"I assure you," Thaddeus Bobrowski told him, "that even
if she were dying, she would be carried out to the carriage."

Luckily Evelina was not yet dying, and Mme Bobrowska
volunteered to accompany her on the journey. She was able
to walk down the steps of the house on her brother's arm
while her little boy waited in the shabby carriage. Halfway
down to the great gate, an open carriage harnessed with
three horses in the Russian fashion was drawn up to watch,
the police captain sitting in it with the visor of his flat cap
pulled down to hide his face.

Evelina arrived in safety at Chernigov; but as the doctors
had foretold, her health grew steadily worse. In February
1865, Apollo wrote that she had been confined to bed for
four months with barely enough strength to look at him or

speak. He could bring her no relief; and while he cared for her or did the errands, little Conrad was inevitably left to fend for himself. Two months later in April 1865, Evelina died.

Apollo continued to write in tones of despair. All he could do for Conrad was shield him from the atmosphere of Chernigov or, in other words, prevent him seeing anybody but his father. There was no comfort anywhere, and even letters caused such homesickness that they were equivalent to a day of mourning. Actually, Apollo was not entirely sunk in idleness. Books had found their way to him in fair quantities. He could teach his son in Polish and, if he had not the energy for original work, he could at least translate. Accordingly, he produced translations into Polish of excellent quality, mostly of French romantics such as Verlaine or Victor Hugo, and also from Heine and even from Shakespeare. This was of course a silent occupation, and Apollo's companionship was not cheerful for a growing boy. Always moody, he had now become morbidly religious. His devotion to his dead wife approached the point of mania. On anniversaries of her death he spent the whole day saying nothing, eating nothing, and simply gazing at her portrait. Aware that Conrad needed companionship which he could not give him, he was still unable for a year after Evelina's death to send the boy from him.

Apparently, the only protest that Conrad could make against the daily misery of such a life was to break down physically. In the absence of records it is hard to know what was wrong with him — migraine, a nervous stomach, or kidney stones. It may be fairly said, however, that a tendency to

respond to emotional strain with physical illness now began
which was to cause him much suffering in adult life. At all
events, his father was alarmed enough to send him to Novofastov for the summer of 1866, where his health improved
enough for his grandmother to take him back to Chernigov
in October. Predictably, his health broke down again almost
at once, so that he was taken to Kiev by Mme Bobrowska to
visit doctors and returned with her to Novofastov. Here he
had the experience of seeing a real prince ride up to visit in a
traveling carriage mounted on sleigh runners and drawn by
six horses, preceded by a horseman lighting the way with a
blazing ball of tow and resin in an iron basket at the end of
a long stick slung from his saddlebow. Straying into a part
of the house where he was not wanted, the boy discovered
that the prince was sadly old and deaf. All the same, the
old man remembered Grandfather Korzeniowski, with
whom he had fought in the 1830 rebellion, and said that
Conrad was like him. Prince Roman was one of Poland's
many martyrs, brutally treated and sent to the mines by the
Russians when he was discovered in the Polish ranks. The
little boy, shocked to find him so unglamorous, did not know
till later that he had once been as young, rich, and roman-
tically married as a prince in a fairytale.

By the time the boy rejoined his father, Apollo had developed tuberculosis and like Evelina was marked for death.
It became possible to represent to government officials that
he could no longer be a danger to the state. At the end of
1867, he was released to go to Algiers and Madeira for his
health; but he had not money or strength to travel so far.
Crossing the border into Austrian Poland with Conrad, he

moved around to visit friends and went to a mountain resort in search of health. Presently he settled in Lwow for a few months, looking for some way to earn. Ever since his arrest he had been supported by relatives, mainly by the Bobrow-skis, who had also established a small fund for the benefit of Conrad. Finally Apollo was offered an editorial post in Cracow, but proved too ill to work. He took to his bed shortly after his arrival and died a few months later, leaving his penniless orphan to the care of Evelina's relations.

The Bobrowskis did not bring Conrad back to Novofastov because he was a Russian subject and would probably not have been permitted to return to Cracow, where Apollo had wished him to be brought up. The Austrian Empire, com-posed of Czechs, Hungarians, Bohemians, Slovakians, Poles, and Italians as well as Germans, granted cultural tolerance in order to survive. For this reason, in Cracow Conrad could attend a Polish school. In Russia, on the other hand, his par-entage would always count against him. Thus one effect of Apollo's death was to separate the boy from Novofastov, the only home he had ever known. The little school by the Florian Gate had a small boarding department which was kept by the widow Georgeon and her unmarried daughters for country boys who came into Cracow for their schooling. His guardians established him here with boys of his own age, but the widow and her daughters made no substitute for his lost family. The Georgeon school was just another place where he ate and slept, extending into his private life the tiresome disciplines of school.

Even so, when he was freed from the depressing company of his father, Conrad's strength rapidly revived. In the first summer his grandmother took him to Bohemia for his health; but by the time he was fourteen he had made a remarkable recovery from his disastrous childhood. Uncle Thaddeus, guardian to about thirty other children orphaned by the revolt of 1863, kept a special place in his heart for the only son of his beloved sister. He wrote Conrad regular letters of good advice which established him as a father-figure who was at least reliable. Thaddeus was a widower and his daughter Josefina died before she was fifteen, with the consequence that he fussed increasingly about young Conrad's welfare and saw to it that a tutor was found for him because his Latin and Greek were not adequate for admission to St. Jacek's High School. The young man he employed was a student at Cracow University whom Conrad liked and who took charge of him for a couple of summer vacations. Uncle Thaddeus got regular reports from this tutor and urged his nephew to repress impractical Korzeniowski impulses in favor of sensible Bobrowski traits more like his own.

There was no doubt that the boy was temperamental. Lively and popular with his schoolmates, he did not take kindly to the severely classical disciplines of St. Jacek's, where his wide reading and interest in literature were undervalued in face of his deficiencies in Latin and Greek. Besides, the gulf between teacher and pupil was widened by emphasis on the German language and Austrian history, compulsory in the curriculum, but resented by every boy as a patriotic duty.

All the same, by the time that Conrad was fifteen, to the distant eye of Uncle Thaddeus he seemed a reasonably nor-

mal boy, saved by the sensible way in which he had been
handled. There was, for instance, no trace in him of his
father's religious morbidity. Either because his prayers for
dear Papa had not been answered, or simply out of reaction,
he had permanently lost interest in the church which was
bringing him up. St. Jacek's graduated its boys at sixteen,
so that it was time to be thinking about a career. Cracow
University and then perhaps the Austrian civil service seemed
suitable to his uncle. Naturalization as an Austrian should
be easy for a freeman of Cracow, thought Uncle Thaddeus,
who had perhaps inspired the gesture. He was well aware
that it might be dangerous for his nephew to remain Russian.
For one thing, Russian conscription, highly arbitrary in its
selection, posed no threat to the officer class. Conrad's status
as the son of a convict, however, rendered him liable to be
seized for a private soldier and retained indefinitely amid
brutalizing conditions, perhaps for the rest of his life. Small
wonder that Thaddeus was anxious to get his nephew settled
safely in an Austrian career.

To one or two people in his early teens the boy had men-
tioned a fantasy so unreal that he was bound to grow out of
it. Neither Thaddeus nor the rest of the Bobrowskis took it
seriously. Only gradually did it dawn on his outraged kin-
dred that Conrad really was determined to go to sea.

"To sea!"

"To sea?"

The shock circulated among the boy's relations, who were
horrified and uncomprehending. Poles did not go to sea,
for the simple reason that theirs was an inland country. It
did occur to Uncle Thaddeus that Austria, though an inland

empire, had an outlet into the Adriatic and a small fleet based thereon. Well, a career in the Austrian navy might be an odd thing for a Pole, but one never knew what an Austrian admiral might do for Poland. To his dismay, the boy refused to consider this notion. He wanted to sail the oceans of the world, not serve on a gunboat in the Adriatic. Incredibly, the only child of those high-souled patriot martyrs had made up his mind to get away from Poland altogether.

Much moved, Uncle Thaddeus made a journey to Cracow in person, but the discussion was unsatisfactory because neither party understood the state of his own feelings. The boy himself could not explain his craze for adventure. Brought up to reverence the sacrifice of poor Papa and dearest Mama, educated in a Polish school where patriotic sentiments ran high, he was convinced of the sacred nature of Polish ideals. Accused of deserting the cause for which his parents had given their lives, he had little to say except that his nature was not his own fault. His rejection of his surroundings had been made long ago in defense of sanity and reason before he was old enough to know what he was doing. It was purely instinctive with him now.

Thaddeus Bobrowski's position was not much clearer. He was a patriot in the style of his father, keeping up Polish traditions, seeing his wards educated privately rather than in Russian schools, and waiting for the sort of chance which the holocaust of World War I eventually gave Poland. In his inmost heart he had never forgiven Korzeniowski for the disaster he had brought on Evelina by his part in stirring up the hopeless revolt of 1863. On the other hand, Evelina herself was a sainted figure to her brother, while Stefan

Bobrowski had been one of the leading figures of the tragic rising. Thaddeus Bobrowski was too intimately connected with those days to take the desertion of Evelina's son with equanimity. It did not weigh with him that every well-to-do Pole, including the Bobrowskis, had relatives who had gone into exile in Belgium or France, while about three hundred thousand of the poorer Poles were leaving yearly for the United States. Such behavior, understandable in many, was not fitting for the son of his martyred sister.

In the circumstances, Uncle Thaddeus behaved well. He did his best to make the boy feel guilty, but would not absolutely forbid a choice which was essential to his happiness. He only asked that Conrad take time to think things over, working hard meanwhile to get a good final grade at St. Jacek's. He then arranged a European tour for Conrad during the summer in the company of his tutor, hoping that the arguments of that excellent young man would change his purpose.

This wise procedure very nearly succeeded. The tutor took his task seriously, arguing with his pupil in railway trains, on lake steamers, and on steady tramps across the countryside. Gradually the boy weakened and, as they rested at the top of an Alpine pass, felt himself in a mood to give up. To some natures, mountains are a good place for big decisions, inviting them by their wide views and their air of superior calmness. As Conrad wavered they were passed by a small group consisting of an Englishman on foot, his Swiss guide following, and three donkeys carrying two ladies and some baggage.

There was no reason why the Englishman should have

made the slightest difference to an argument which was at
the moment centering on what reward Conrad could expect
in honor or conscience when he came to the end of his days.
It happened, however, that the boy who sat by the roadside
possessed an extraordinary power of perceiving something
memorable in the most casual of human contacts. In this
case it was the "inextinguishable and comic ardor" with
which this Alpine enthusiast advanced that struck his fancy.
The Englishman's innocent satisfaction with himself, mankind, and mountain scenery elicited a faint smile even from
the tutor. To the boy, the stranger's appearance was a voice
on the side of sanity, indicating another man who liked to
see the world and did so with a good conscience, blamed by
no one.

The tutor felt his defeat. He picked up his knapsack.
"You are an incorrigible, hopeless Don Quixote. That's what
you are," he said. For a few minutes he walked ahead in
silence and then, letting the boy come up with him, he put
his hand on Conrad's shoulder. "Well, that's enough. We
will have no more of it." The issue was settled.

Uncle Thaddeus's instinct was to put plans off, doubtless
reasoning that Conrad was absurdly young at sixteen to fend
for himself. Accordingly he removed him to Lwow, where
a distant cousin ran a boardinghouse for orphans of the revolt of 1863. Presumably some arrangement was made for
him to pursue a course of study, but the most important
thing he apparently did was to fall in love with his cousin's
daughter Tekla, who enjoyed tormenting him both privately
and publicly to such an extent that he came out of the experience with an abiding distrust of himself in relation to

Joseph Conrad at sixteen

women. He had been brought up entirely with boys or men, and though three of his school friends had a sister whom he had admired rather distantly for her nobly patriotic soul, it seems that Tekla was his first real experience with a girl since his cousin Josefina.

Conrad's remarks about this early love are so disjointed that we cannot be quite sure that Tekla was the heroine of this incident. It seems likely, however, that Tekla's family, annoyed by the whole affair, were anxious to get rid of Conrad, forcing Thaddeus to consider whether experience of life at sea might not be better for his nephew than hanging around and getting into mischief. He therefore shouldered the burden of making a practical arrangement. Conrad, he perceived, would have to be apprenticed to the sailor's trade in France, since Austria had no seaborne traffic to speak of, except in her Italian possessions. The boy spoke fluent French, but no Italian, while France was a country in which every Pole of good family in those days could find connections. After some correspondence, one was discovered who had actually entered the French marine service. Victor Chodzko was starting on a long voyage, but a French friend of his called Baptistin Solary wrote from Marseilles to assure Uncle Thaddeus that if his nephew really had a hankering after the dog's life of a sailor, he would be happy to see he got onto a decent ship. Though it must have occurred to Uncle Thaddeus that a boy not quite seventeen was rather young to start out entirely alone in a fresh country, the circumstances allowed him little choice. He contented himself with making prudent arrangements. Mme Bobrowska, who had recently died, had left a small legacy to her grandson. His uncle took charge of this and, adding it to the fund already established for Conrad, arranged to pay him a modest annual allowance. Supplied with a few letters of introduction and fortified by exhortations to work hard and not take after the Korzeniowskis, young Conrad set out for adventure by train to Marseilles.

SECOND LIFE

The Sea Wanderer

3

Wild Oats in Marseilles

THE MORNING AFTER Conrad arrived in Marseilles, Baptistin Solary breezed into the hotel where the boy was sleeping off a tedious journey and, flinging the shutters wide to let in the sun, announced cheerfully that he had better be up and ready for a three-year voyage to the South Seas. This, however, was merely a joke. Solary, who had quit seafaring to make a better living ashore, seems to have thought that with a little more knowledge of his chosen profession, Conrad would change his mind. Instead of making any particular effort to find a ship, he introduced the boy to his own connections in Marseilles.

Baptistin Solary was a short, dark young man with a high complexion and a lively manner who was related to an enormous circle of shipwrights, pilots, sailmakers, ship chandlers, master stevedores, and other people who earned their living in the port of Marseilles. He lost no time in making Conrad known to those of his friends who had the most direct connection with the sea, namely the pilots, who went out on regular patrols to wait for ships which wanted to enter the harbor.

The pilots took to the boy with enthusiasm, adopting him as a kind of mascot. Finding a difficulty with the name Korzeniowski which was to be shared by sailors around the world, they christened him "the little friend of Baptistin," or "the friend" for short. They let him come out on patrol with them, handle an occasional rope, and as a great thrill take the tiller on moonlit nights when there was not too much wind in the big sail. They showed him what it meant to go out in all weathers in a half-decked boat and taught him to pull an oar in the skiff which went alongside an incoming ship to put a pilot aboard. He listened to their tales and fingered the brass button which one old grandfather kept on his coat in memory of service in the French navy in 1830 under the last king of the old Bourbon line. To a student fresh from a classical education, this ancient port of Marseilles brought romantic dreams of the wanderings of Odysseus, of Carthaginian galleys or Roman pleasure boats. Decidedly Solary was wrong about Conrad, while Uncle Thaddeus was bound to have more trouble with that impractical Korzeniowski blood. The boy was having the time of his life, finding the matter-of-fact routine of the pilots pure romance.

Meanwhile, there were his letters of introduction which brought him a connection in social circles more appropriate for a Polish gentleman. M. Delestang, a merchant trading with the West Indies, has been preserved by the unkind pen of his young acquaintance as a gray formal man who seemed to have been born permanently into his middle fifties. Politically, he was an extreme conservative in a period when the future government of France was anybody's guess. Only three years earlier the Franco-Prussian war had put an end to the rule of Napoleon III in France and established the German Empire, profoundly altering the balance of power in Europe. After savage fighting between the Right and Left in Paris, a French Republic had been set up which, like all governments born out of a national defeat, was widely unpopular. M. Delestang was a monarchist who favored the claim of the Comte de Chambord, representative of the old Bourbon line; and it is notable that the President of the French Republic himself had strong leanings in the same direction. Mme Delestang, slightly better born than her husband, had social ambitions. She held receptions in her big, gloomy drawing room for people who habitually referred to the glorious reign of Louis XIV, two hundred years before, as the age of gold.

Neither of the Delestangs was of a temperament to appeal to a boy of seventeen, but they were kind to him. M. Delestang, Conrad says, was his banker, which meant that he called regularly at the private office as well as the counting house downstairs, receiving messages of regards to send to his "honored uncle." Mme Delestang invited him into her carriage for formal drives and occasionally to her salon, where he heard gossip about the royal claimants to the thrones of France and Spain. After a couple of months, as the boy persisted in his desire to become a seaman, he was allowed to make a voyage to the West Indies in the *Mont-*

Blanc belonging to Delestang, an elderly ship which, running before a Gulf of Lyons gale "leaked fully, generously, overflowingly, all over — like a basket." He was registered as a passenger, but probably paid nothing, taking his turn at the pumps or wherever he could be useful.

It was not a glorious start, and one wonders whether Solary had found difficulty in placing a boy who before he reached Marseilles had only laid eyes on the sea once or twice, and then from a distance. The *Mont-Blanc* was a twenty-two-year-old wooden sailing bark of no great size which carried a mixed cargo to Martinique and other West Indian ports, returning with sugar or logwood, a type of wood useful in making dyes for printed cottons. Conrad's maiden voyage started in December 1874, about a week after his seventeenth birthday, and lasted till the end of May 1875. No special incidents marked it, but this hardly mattered when everything was a new adventure, including the work and discipline of the crew, the vicissitudes of weather, black faces in the West Indies, even the tiresome processes of stowing or unloading cargo. In any event, Conrad did well enough to be off again after a month in port, this time as a regular apprentice.

Since the latter half of 1875 was stormy, the old *Mont-Blanc*, limping into Le Havre on the 23rd of December, had taken a real battering. Conrad had been exposed to the tremendous demands on strength and stamina which sailing ships very often made on their crews. In later life he would comment to his friends on the ridiculousness of his choice of profession. "Look at me!" he would exclaim, spreading his hands. "Was I built to handle heavy ropes and spars?" With a shrug of his shoulders he would dismiss the folly of so small a man trying to pit his strength against the fury of the elements. At least he was broad-shouldered and powerful for his size when his frame had fully developed. At seventeen, he had only the energy of youth to compensate for a physical inadequacy which would remain a problem.

In any event, he had by now had enough of the old *Mont-Blanc*. A few years earlier Delestang had chartered a new bark called the *Saint-Antoine*, which naturally attracted his top captain and crew. Conrad got the promise of a berth on her next voyage; but unfortunately she had just set out on her West Indian round, so that the transfer involved a six-month wait in Marseilles. Conrad wrote virtuously to Uncle Thaddeus that he was going to spend his time in studies necessary to his profession. No doubt he did learn with the aid of Solary's connections, but his circle of acquaintance soon began to spread farther than the port. There were five famous restaurants in a row on the Cannebière, which was the main street of the Marseilles old quarter. Each had its "habituals" who gathered casually for conversation over a dinner, a glass of wine, or a cup of coffee. Prices were not high, and it was natural that Conrad experimented with them.

Marseilles was the greatest city of Provence, that part of France which borders on the Mediterranean and possesses a characteristic local culture which has flourished since the Middle Ages — and indeed back into Roman times. There were in Conrad's day a Marseilles art school and several newspapers on which young men of talent had found employment. In fact, there was a "Bohemian" set of artists and

writers, centering around some older men who were nation-
ally famous. It is not probable that these last took any notice
of the slight, dark Polish boy with the high cheekbones and
slanted eyes and perhaps the faint beginnings of that pointed
beard and wide mustache which he wore through adult life.
Nevertheless, Apollo Korzeniowski had handed down to his
son a taste for literature and an interest in French writers.
There were younger men on the fringes of the group who
would admit him to their circle when he walked into the
restaurant where they gathered.

All this was harmless and not even very expensive. The
boy hardly drank at all and had no tendency to dissipation.
It did, however, throw him into the society of people who
treated him as older than he was. Curiously enough, moreover, while he was consorting with what was essentially a
liberal set, he was also widening his acquaintance in the
social circles of Mme Delestang. This lady's personal friends
were much too old for him, but some of her occasional visitors were younger and deeply involved in the civil war which
was currently going on between rival claimants for the
throne of Spain. There was no reason why the boy should
care who ruled in Spain; but he did like adventure. Some
of the men who had been across the border in the service of
the Pretender brought back exciting stories.

Few of these varied contacts were reflected in the letters
he wrote to Uncle Thaddeus, in reply to his lectures about
working hard and not overspending his allowance. No
doubt it had always been this way. There was a certain level,
both in Cracow and Marseilles, on which he communicated
with a revered but distant guardian. In Cracow, Thaddeus

had received reports from school or tutor, but information about his nephew in Marseilles was harder to come by.

It soon became evident that Conrad's modest means required an economy which was difficult to practice during a long stay ashore. By April he had anticipated his allowance as far ahead as the following October and said that he had lent the money to friends. In May and in July he telegraphed for more, further infuriating his uncle because Novofastov was twenty-eight miles from the telegraph office, so that to deliver any message was a considerable expense. Before he sailed on the *Saint-Antoine* on July 8, Conrad asked his uncle to repay 165 francs to a M. Bonnard, who was perhaps a moneylender. Uncle Thaddeus took care of most of such matters with money which had been left by relatives for his nephew's use and was somewhat consoled by letters from the captain of the *Mont-Blanc* and from M. Delestang giving the boy a good character. But this did not prevent him from delivering a long and serious lecture, which he addressed to Delestang too late to reach the culprit before his departure for the West Indies. At least the young man would be out of mischief during the voyage; and, though he was signed on as "steward," he was really acting as junior officer.

There were three other officers and thirteen men as well as a passenger aboard the *Saint-Antoine*. She was much the same size as the *Mont-Blanc*, but only six years old and in good condition. On her, Conrad struck up a friendship with a seaman who was to remain in some ways his ideal of the adventurous man. Dominic Cervoni, mate of the *Saint-Antoine*, was a Corsican sailor of about forty, a broad-chested man with black hair and thick, black, curled mustaches who faced every emergency with the same imperturbable decision. Underneath his quiet manner, Dominic was an astute and ruthless personality who could outthink an opponent with as little effort as it cost him to do the right thing in a crisis. He was, in fact, a modern Odysseus, a sea wanderer brought up in the smuggling trade with many strange stories of loves, and dangers, and bloodshed to tell, a massive character, equal to anything. He had perhaps the sum of many qualities which Conrad had admired in great explorers and appeared to the boy's fascinated eyes the sort of person he would have liked to be. Cervoni had a single drawback in the shape of a nephew César, whose father had killed a man in a vendetta and taken to the bush to dodge the gendarmes. This made it Dominic's duty to make a man out of César, and seldom can anyone have had more unpromising material. Conrad described César as physically revolting, untruthful, impudent, and venomous. Dominic's remedy for his faults was to knock him down, which he did fairly often with a sweep of his great arm, disregarding the horrible look of impotent rage which César gave him in return. Privately Dominic admitted to Conrad that the boy did not like the sea and wanted to be a locksmith. "To learn how to pick locks, I suppose," he added bitterly.

"Why not let him be a locksmith?"

"Who would teach him?" Dominic demanded. "Where could I leave him?" His voice dropped in despair. "He steals, you know, alas! *Par la Madone*! I believe he would put poison in your food and mine — the viper!"

Possibly Conrad embroidered this conversation, but he undoubtedly felt a deep revulsion for the nephew, even though his admiration for the uncle grew. Both feelings were to have their effect on his immediate future, while Dominic Cervoni was to appear in Conrad's fiction time and again, unmistakable in the different settings in which the novelist placed him.

St. Pierre, the port of Martinique, was already familiar to Conrad as a town of southern French charm, not unlike old New Orleans, though in a more tropical setting. It was, however, a hazardous port in which to linger in hurricane season between mid-July and mid-October; and in any case the *Saint-Antoine* had urgent business elsewhere. Though presumably she did not advertise the fact, she was carrying arms to the insurgents of a South American republic which was involved in civil war. This seems to have been Colombia, on the Caribbean Sea, which had been for seventy years in a state of turmoil, typical of South American unrest. A liberal government, in power for the last fifteen years, had succeeded in separating church and state and establishing secular control of public education. This was a step which the conservatives were now determined to reverse by a revolution. Not a few of the old families had connections in France who may have been known to the conservative M. Delestang and may partly explain why so proper a personage had engaged in a traffic which, though considered a fair game by enterprising North Americans, had certainly its dubious side.

War had broken out in Colombia that very August, and the rebels had already been defeated in one battle by the time the *Saint-Antoine* arrived at Cartagena, once headquarters of the Spanish Inquisition and still the stronghold of the con-

servatives. The actual port of Cartagena was no more than a
hamlet without modern quays. Ships anchored offshore in
windless waters protected from the Caribbean by three unin-
habited islets. From here, the *Saint-Antoine* unloaded into
flat-bottomed lighters, which in turn transferred their cargo
into mule carts. Going ashore, Conrad found Cartagena to
be a walled Spanish city of about 14,000 lying a few miles inland on a flat plain and at the moment in a state of considerable tension. A second battle was impending, for which the
arms of the *Saint-Antoine* had arrived in the nick of time.
Not unnaturally, the *Saint-Antoine*'s crew were caught up in
the popular emotion so that, even though the issues at stake
were of no importance to them, they followed the struggle
with a sense of having picked their team. It is probably this
feeling that impressed the country vividly on Conrad's imagination with its windless gulf and its flat plain, behind which
rose the majestic rampart of the Cordilleras, whose lofty
plateaus and high passes were swept by icy winds or shrouded
in mist. There were gold and silver in those inaccessible
rocks; and the beginnings of development with the aid of
foreign investment included a railroad being constructed
largely by Italian labor. Some three months later, Conrad
read of the final defeat of the rebels at Los Chancos, news
of which had been held up by the rebel siege of Buenaventura, terminal of the cable to Panama and Colombia's sole
means of quick communication. To Buenaventura the government had rushed its single warship with reinforcements.

Long before these events, the *Saint-Antoine* had touched
at a couple of ports in Venezuela, in both of which Conrad
went briefly ashore. He was never to visit South America

again; and yet on the basis of these few weeks of experience, fortified by general reading, he constructed many years afterward his most ambitious novel, which even included the troubles at Buenaventura, so detailed was his memory of the past.

The ship went back to St. Pierre, but did not linger to take on cargo because hurricanes were known to be close. She left for St. Thomas in the Virgin Islands, which she found a shambles after the worst hurricane in fifty years. However, she managed to take on coal for Port-au-Prince and sailed in that direction, calculating on a voyage of eight days. Caught in an even more violent hurricane than that which had torn up St. Thomas, she arrived a week late, but still afloat, to find Haiti likewise in a state of revolution. Santo Domingo close by was also in turmoil, while Cuba on the other side was in the eighth year of a war of independence against Spain. Disturbed conditions attracted strange characters, and Conrad was already storing a gallery of portraits in his retentive mind.

In Haiti he received a letter from Uncle Thaddeus, to whom he had written asking if he was to be cut off in silence forever for his sins. Thaddeus was too fond of his nephew not to respond, but his continued annoyance expressed itself in a series of carping criticisms. "Last year you lost your trunk," he reminded Conrad angrily. "What else was there to think about on your journey but yourself and your belongings?" A year earlier when the *Mont-Blanc* had limped into Le Havre in such a condition that extensive repairs were needed before she could get back to Marseilles, Conrad had returned there by train. This was probably as inexpensive as lingering in Le Havre; but somehow or other he had lost his trunk, containing not only his family photographs but apparently such things of vital importance as his birth certificate. Uncle Thaddeus, who had probably never misplaced anything in his life, had no conception of what conditions must have been like on the old *Mont-Blanc* or the muddle which must have ensued. Peevishly he went on to complain about the slovenliness of his nephew's letters. "Can't you have a supply of paper and write in an orderly manner?" he inquired of the young man who had just sailed through the worst hurricane in living memory. His letters had so strong a tendency to degenerate into this kind of criticism that it is quite surprising that Conrad continued to be fond of him. But though in later life he was too proud to accept verbal criticisms, Conrad was inwardly a self-doubter, quick to blame himself at disparagement conveyed by letter, especially by anybody he was fond of. On this occasion, though he knew he had been seriously to blame, he could hardly have helped reflecting that it was no use trying to make Uncle understand a sailor's life.

In February 1877, the *Saint-Antoine* got back to Marseilles, where Conrad found waiting for him an immensely long letter, almost a book, from his uncle, recounting his extravagances in detail. The boy had offered to repay his debt out of the allowance, but Uncle Thaddeus dismissed this as impossible. He would not leave his nephew destitute, which would merely force him to run up more debts. In fact, he concluded, for the first and for the last time he was willing to put the whole down to youthful folly, and forgive. For his own son, he said, he would not have done it; but he could

not refuse a last chance to the son of his sister and the grandson of his mother, who had so lately died. Conrad must
write him and tell him how he had profited by the voyage
of the *Saint-Antoine*. Did the captain give him lessons? Was
he studying English, or perhaps some other language? Had
he recovered the trunk he lost in Le Havre with his papers
in it? In sum, what about his moral and physical well-being?

How Conrad answered this letter is not recorded, but
when the *Saint-Antoine* went out again, he was not with her.
He later told his uncle that he was laid up at the time with
an anal abscess; but, at all events, he faced the prospect of
another half-year of idleness in Marseilles until the *Saint-
Antoine* got back into port. After a while, Uncle Thaddeus
received a letter saying that the *Saint-Antoine* was going to
make a three-year voyage around the world. Could Conrad
have an advance on his allowance to cover equipment? Uncle
Thaddeus sent him one, and then a second, reminded by
Conrad that he would not be in a position to collect his
allowance for a long time and must take money with him.

It is sad to record that there was no truth whatever in this
story, and very likely none in the young man's account of
having lent his allowance to friends in the preceding year.
He had taken his uncle's solemn warning to heart only to the
extent of understanding that appeals for money would produce results only when accompanied by a plausible tale. We
may guess that Uncle Thaddeus was reaping what he had
sown, and that Conrad's practice of extracting sums on false
pretenses may have dated back to his school days. Growing
up involves every normal boy in troubles with which his
family has to cope. If Conrad had spent his allowance un-

wisely at St. Jacek's or in buying presents for Tekla in Lwow, how could he have explained his problems to an uncle whom he never saw? Conrad was not naturally untruthful, but he was inventive. In 1877, he was still under twenty and influenced by people who treated him as mature. Being, despite his uncle's exhortations, a Korzeniowski, he had a weakness for schemes to make his fortune which involved the sort of risk of which Uncle Thaddeus would never approve. To carry out his present plan, he needed cash; hence the mythical voyage of the *Saint-Antoine*. It is fair to say that some of the money he extracted from his uncle was in trust for him, left by various relations. For the rest, he was anticipating his allowance in the expectation of making a profit.

Uncle Thaddeus paid out unsuspiciously three thousand francs and left Novofastov for the agricultural fair at Kiev early in 1878, serenely confident that Conrad had started with the *Saint-Antoine* on her long voyage. While here, he received two alarming communications. The first was a further demand from M. Bonnard for a thousand francs which he had lent to Conrad. The second was a telegram from Richard Fecht, whom he knew by name as one of Conrad's friends. It said laconically: CONRAD WOUNDED. SEND MONEY. COME. He went, camouflaging the shock by intense irritation that the boy should have chosen the time of the fair to get into trouble.

The story subsequently told by Bobrowski in a letter to an old friend of Conrad's father differs a good deal from the accounts of the same incident given by Conrad in his writings. There being no proof one way or the other, biographers have taken sides according to their feelings, supporting their positions either by guesswork or by a series of details which are not conclusive. Almost certainly, Bobrowski gave the tale as he understood it, but did Conrad confide completely in his uncle? Before making up our own minds, we ought to consider how far what Conrad wrote may be taken as a reliable guide to the facts of his life.

Conrad was primarily a fiction writer, even though much of his material came from his own experience. One or two of his stories come so close to what actually happened that they seem at first sight literal truth. No one, however, could classify "Youth" or "The Shadow Line" as anything but fiction, because their artistic effect is evidently the result of deep reflection. We can see that the arrangement of these stories is deliberate and must suppose that events have been selected to prove a point, that details here and there may have been invented or transposed from some other voyage. Thus, even in such tales it is hard to draw a fixed line between what is factual and what is merely true to the spirit of Conrad's narrative.

When Conrad moves to nonfiction, the change is in some respects not great. *The Mirror of the Sea* is not an autobiographical account of Conrad's sea adventures, but a series of essays on what the sea meant to him, illustrated freely by anecdotes from his own experience. Conrad invariably spoke of *The Mirror of the Sea* as a work of art. Thus, though he defended it as true to the spirit of his sea life, it may not follow that every story therein occurred precisely as he tells it. He might protect his privacy in details or twist events to make a better story, while yet insisting that *The Mirror of the Sea* was essentially truth. Since the crisis which brought Uncle Thaddeus to Marseilles in such a hurry is recounted in *The Mirror of the Sea* and in *The Arrow of Gold,* a piece of Conrad's later fiction, we shall probably never know what happened for certain and must content ourselves with probabilities.

Uncle Thaddeus's story is clear, but it looks as though he may have been confused on detail, perhaps by Conrad himself, or possibly by his ignorance of most of the people concerned. Conrad, he says, had been engaged in smuggling goods into Spain in partnership with Captain Duteuil of the *Mont-Blanc.* More probably, as we shall see, it was Dominic Cervoni. The illegality of his proceedings did not worry the boy much because France and Spain were both foreign countries to him. He invested a thousand francs and made a profit of four hundred. Encouraged, he put in everything he could lay his hands on and lost it all. Captain Duteuil (or perhaps Cervoni) left for Buenos Aires; but Conrad could not go too because he was now over twenty and would at twenty-one be liable for military service as a Russian subject. French law forbade the shipping of aliens in such circumstances, so that permanent employment in the French marine was impossible. This story sounds fairly plausible until we remember that Conrad had eleven months to go before he became twenty-one and could easily have taken passage on a French ship for less than that period.

Penniless, in debt, and without a profession, Conrad — again according to Uncle Thaddeus — borrowed eight hundred francs from Richard Fecht in order to get to Villefranche to join the American navy. There are improbabilities about this, too; but Thaddeus may have been confused about the status of the American ship the boy wanted to join. The detail is not important because on the way Conrad dropped in at Monte Carlo to recoup his fortunes. Losing the whole eight hundred francs, he returned to Marseilles more desperate than ever. He invited Fecht to tea to explain, but, unable to face him, tried to commit suicide by shooting himself through the heart. Luckily the bullet did not hit any vital spot, so that by the time his uncle arrived, he was already on his feet. Thaddeus adds that inquiry showed the boy had no real vices and that both friends and employers spoke well of him.

Before we comment on this story, let us look at Conrad's account of the same affair, mostly from *The Mirror of the Sea*. According to Conrad, he was smuggling arms on behalf of Don Carlos, the current pretender to the throne of Spain. In other words, he was interfering in a quarrel which had started over forty years before when the King of Spain died, leaving the succession to his daughter Isabella, then aged three. There was some question about whether a woman could legally inherit the throne of Spain, and Isabella's uncle Carlos was convinced that he was the true heir. An ardent and conservative Catholic, Carlos stood for the absolute rule of the church in education, exemption of its wealth from taxation, and even the return of the Inquisition. The strength of his movement lay in the country parts where the influence of the village priests was very strong. The Basque provinces at the foot of the Pyrenees being of this nature, the cause of Don Carlos also became associated there with local freedom from restrictions imposed by Madrid. These provinces, moreover, were nearest to France and easiest for the Carlists to influence from exile.

The partisans of Isabella won the struggle; but Don Carlos died convinced that he was the true king, leaving his claims to his descendants. The present Don Carlos, grandson of the original man, found his opportunity when Isabella was driven into exile in 1868, leaving one son, Alfonso, who was, as everybody well knew, not the son of her husband. Eight years of chaos followed, during which the cause of Don Carlos prospered, forcing his opponents to rally, whether they liked it or not, around Alfonso. In 1872, Don Carlos established himself on Spanish soil, effective master of a great deal of northern Spain. He made a fine-looking king, tall, youngish, and impressively bearded. Unfortunately he lacked qualities of leadership, preferred setting up a court to directing an army, and amused himself by playing unpleasant practical jokes on influential supporters. In March 1876, he was forced out of Spain and published a proclamation asking his followers to refrain from useless bloodshed in support of his cause.

Since this was the case, what was Conrad doing smuggling arms to Carlists in 1877, more than a year after Don Carlos had given up? His own statements are fairly precise. He says that a certain Lord X, whom one biographer guesses may have been the Duke of Norfolk, England's leading Catholic and a personal friend of Don Carlos, had chartered a steamship in England to bring arms for the insurgents. These presumably were consigned to a fake company in France. If it is true that Lord X was actually Norfolk, he was putting himself in a very awkward position because his

uncle was currently British ambassador to France. He may
therefore have been particularly anxious to keep the delivery
of his consignments secret. At all events, a cousin of X, together with a local French landowner and an American
soldier of fortune called Blunt who was in Don Carlos's
service, joined with Conrad to buy a sixty-ton vessel which
he called the *Tremolino* for the purpose of the actual smuggling. Of this syndicate of owners, only Conrad, who as-
sumed the name of M. George for the purpose, sailed in the
Tremolino. The rest of the crew was made up by Dominic
Cervoni, his inevitable nephew César, and four other seamen.
They sailed openly from Marseilles with a load of oranges,
made a rendezvous at sea to pick up their contraband, threw
the oranges overboard at their convenience, and delivered
the rifles at night on desolate stretches of the coast, com-
municating with their allies on shore by signal lanterns. Up
to a point, Conrad says, things did go well, though the
Spanish coast guard was unpleasantly active. If any hitch
occurred, they went ashore as an innocent orange boat to
make other arrangements, while M. George carried a money
belt with about three hundred gold pieces, presumably for
judicious bribery. Exactly how the *Tremolino* was paid,
and by whom, is not clear, but the venture was profitable
both to the partners and to the crew who took the risks.
Conrad further suggests that his own personal motive was
neither money nor the cause but love of a lady in Marseilles
with Carlist convictions.

On one occasion when they went ashore in Spain, César
Cervoni disappeared mysteriously but briefly to take his
revenge on his uncle by sending a warning to the coast

guard. When the *Tremolino* put in to make her delivery, the coast-guard boat was waiting for her. She tried to slip away, but was fairly trapped. While there was yet time, Cervoni told M. George to sink the evidence that would land them in a Spanish jail by wrecking the *Tremolino* on the rocks. She was Conrad's first ship and a real beauty, but he knew that Cervoni was right and did the deed. In the midst of the crisis, however, it had occurred to both him and Dominic that César must have betrayed them. Once the idea presented itself, the fact was obvious. With his usual furious gesture, Dominic knocked the traitor clear overboard. They were not far from shore, but César was weighted with the money belt which he had stolen from Conrad's cabin. It sank him like a stone, while the rest of the *Tremolino*'s crew escaped to shore. Partisans hid them and passed them gradually back to France. To Dominic, this conduct by a member of his family was a personal disgrace. Unable to face his friend, he went away — maybe to Buenos Aires.

It is easy to pick holes in this tale or to support it. Don Carlos was not fighting in Spain at this time; but in spite of his proclamation of 1876 he had not given up. It is not impossible that his friends were laying up weapons for another effort. Conrad, who certainly represents the fight as still going on, may be doing so merely to heighten the excitement of an adventure which he actually had. On the other hand, Dominic Cervoni was signed on as mate of the *Saint-Antoine* for nearly all of 1877 and could not apparently have sailed in the *Tremolino* till late in that year. It has been suggested that M. Delestang, smuggler of arms and supporter of reactionary causes, had consented to conceal what Dominic was doing by continuing his name on the roster of the *Saint-Antoine*. Another difficulty is that César Cervoni was alive twenty-eight years later and captain of a coasting vessel. If Conrad actually thought him drowned, he was mistaken.

At all events, Conrad came back to Marseilles after losing the *Tremolino* and all the money he had invested in her. From this moment, Uncle Thaddeus's story about borrowing from Fecht, losing money in Monte Carlo, and attempting suicide can be fitted in. In *The Arrow of Gold,* however, which though fiction has an autobiographical base, Conrad claims that M. George's love affair gave rise to a duel between himself and Blunt, the American soldier of fortune who was one of the group that had bought the *Tremolino.* It is also the case that Conrad's wife and children always believed that the scar on his chest was the result of a duel.

The identity of the lady, if there was one, had best be left until a discussion of *The Arrow of Gold* and its place in Conrad's fiction. But did Conrad attempt suicide or fight a duel? Supporters of the duel theory point out that Blunt was a real man, grandson of Francis Scott Key. Since Conrad often inserts real people into his stories, this by itself proves nothing. Thaddeus, though admitting the suicide attempt in a confidential letter, did spread the duel story around the Bobrowski connections. Was he hushing up a suicide scandal which he admitted to a man who took a special interest in Conrad; or was he concealing the duel from this particular man, because he disapproved of dueling? These and similar questions can be answered one way and another, while the easiest solution is not necessarily the correct one. But if Thaddeus did cover up a suicide attempt by pretending a duel, he must have ordered his nephew to back up his story. Then, in later life, when Conrad married a much younger woman, it would have been embarrassing to tell her the truth when all his relations had heard about the duel. Conrad would have said, "A duel, my dear," without a qualm, reflecting that what had happened in another life in a different country, when she was about five, was none of her business. There is really no proof either way, though it certainly seems likely that Thaddeus told the truth as he understood it when he wrote to Apollo's old friend. For this reason it seems fair to lean to the suicide theory, though all that the evidence actually shows is that young Conrad was not a model boy who had risen miraculously above a disastrous childhood and an unguided adolescence. He was a far more complex character than Uncle Thaddeus had ever foreseen.

4

Fresh Start in England

Uncle Thaddeus paid his nephew's debts, even including his back rent, though he found waste of money particularly hard to forgive. Thaddeus was a careful man, but less well off than his father, partly because of money paid out to his sister and brothers, and partly, no doubt, because times were difficult in Poland. He did not fail to reproach his nephew with the expense and inconvenience of his journey, the current rate of exchange, and the awkward timing of the crisis. Such annoyances, however, did not prevent him from going to the root of the matter: Conrad was doing no good in Marseilles and would be well advised to come back to Austrian Poland in order to settle down in a respectable occupation.

Conrad refused to quit the sea and was able to show his uncle that his record in his profession had been good. He consented, however, to make a fresh start, probably suggesting the British merchant marine, where no questions would be asked about Russian military service. With considerable generosity, Bobrowski increased the allowance which had proved insufficient, while Conrad got a temporary job in the port to tide him over until a suitable English ship should make its appearance. Within a few months, he found a berth on the British steamer *Mavis,* which had touched at Marseilles on her way to Constantinople, apparently paying a small sum to rank as an apprentice officer. Either conditions were not as they had been represented, or else he simply did not like the *Mavis.* At all events, when she touched at Lowestoft in England, he left her immediately and went to London, where he tried in vain to get another ship. Since he had no connections and spoke only a little English, what money he had was very soon exhausted, and he wrote his uncle anxiously for advice.

Thaddeus refused to advise him or even send him money. Conrad was where he was by his own choice and in circumstances which he had created for himself. Why had he not stayed on the *Mavis?* Who told him to go up to London and spend his money there? He, Thaddeus, had no money for drones and no intention of working so that other people might enjoy themselves at his expense.

This treatment drove Conrad back to Lowestoft, where perhaps some of the *Mavis*'s crew may have had connections. His prospects on arrival in this, his third adopted country, were far less favorable than they had been in Marseilles. He had little money in his pocket, no real friends, and spoke the language with difficulty. It is, indeed, remarkable that though his French accent was flawless, Conrad never spoke like an Englishman, retaining for the rest of his life a thick foreign accent and a habit of underlining his meaning by gestures. His very dark hair and eyes, his triangular face emphasized by a pointed beard, his high cheekbones and slanting eyes gave him an appearance more usual in Mediterranean ports than in England. His name, misspelled in almost every ship's roster for the next eleven years, was unintelligible to English people. The excessive number of his Christian names led him to use first one, then another, "Joseph" and "Conrad" being favorites, presumably because they were easy to recognize in English.

Having lost the premium which he had paid to the *Mavis,* he realized that his uncle would not start him afresh. He would have to approach his problems in a practical spirit and begin from the bottom. Accordingly he decided to improve his English and learn about his new environment before he made another attempt in London. He therefore took a job on a coasting vessel which may have been built for some romantic purpose, since her name was the *Skimmer of the Seas.* If so, she had come down in the world, since her present occupation was to go up to Newcastle and bring back coal for the Lowestoft pottery works. Ten weeks of coaling gave Conrad sufficient confidence in his English to write a careful letter in answer to an advertisement in the London *Times* as follows: "SEA — WANTED, respectable YOUTHS for voyage or term in two splendid ships for Australia and others for India, etc. W. Sutherland, 11 Fenchurch Buildings, Fenchurch Street . . ." Washing off accumulated coal and putting on one of the suits he had bought in Marseilles, Conrad invested in a ticket to London.

Perhaps he had never taken a cab in his life, for Marseilles, though a town of considerable size, had supplied what he needed within the area of the old port. At all events, after studying a map, he decided to find Fenchurch Street on foot with the aid of simple navigation. He was lucky to succeed because his accent made him determine not to ask strangers the way, while Fenchurch Buildings were inside a courtyard hidden by a narrow archway, a typical bit of old London. W. Sutherland was discovered to be a heavy-featured man with curly white hair in an office undusted for about fifty years and sufficiently gloomy at one in the afternoon to need the light from a gas jet which hung from the blackened ceiling. As Conrad walked in, he was standing at a high Victorian desk to eat a mutton chop which had been sent in from a restaurant around the corner.

Sutherland recognized his correspondent from Lowestoft, but started to explain that he could do nothing for him. The advertisement in the *Times* had been intended to attract apprentices who would pay a premium to be trained as officers. There was actually a law forbidding the recruitment of ordinary seamen, presumably passed to discourage kidnaping. "Of course I see that you are a gentleman," said W. Sutherland, regarding the trim figure before him, whose shore clothes always emphasized his social standing. "But your wish is to get a berth before the mast."

Taking an interest in a situation which was evidently unusual, Sutherland consented to see whether the law could be, if not quite broken, then at least a little bent to suit the occasion. As a result, Conrad shortly found himself a deck hand on one of the "splendid ships for Australia," namely the *Duke of Sutherland,* a wool clipper of 1047 tons with a crew of twenty-six. She sailed in the middle of October 1878 for Sydney, a voyage of nearly three months and a half without touching land.

Conrad's voyages on the ships of Delestang must have already inured him to many of the hardships of sea life; but as an apprentice or assistant to the officers, he had not been quite on a level with the crew. A berth before the mast was a step down in his profession, besides which he was now thrown together with men whose language he spoke badly. In the following years he was to learn even more about loneliness than the circumstances of his childhood had taught him.

Life on sailing ships had always been exacting, but in Conrad's day competition with steamships was forcing fresh economies on owners, inevitably at the expense of the crew. The pay of a man before the mast had hardly risen for the better part of a century, so that it barely covered the cost of his sea chest and secondhand oilskins. Paid off at the end of a voyage, men shipped out promptly because they could not afford to live ashore. Even a stopover in some port was apt to be too expensive for a common sailor, who spent his pay in one or two nights on the town and was on the lookout for another ship almost at once. Conrad, who received no money from his uncle beyond his allowance and a present of a few pounds sent out to Sydney, was given the job of night watchman in that port, apparently because he had nowhere else to go and so stuck by the ship. The *Duke of Sutherland* lay five months in Sydney harbor waiting for cargo and passengers, during which time Conrad generally went little further than the end of the quay, where stalls sold meals for sixpence. Meanwhile, on shipboard food and water were rationed, while supplies were of the very simplest: bread, weak tea or coffee with sugar, salt beef or salt pork four days a week, with pea soup and potatoes for the other three. The crew had no washing facilities, no heat in any weather, no privacy, not even anywhere to dry their clothes. Men worked for twelve hours a day in ordinary weather and till they dropped in storms. When the *Duke of Sutherland* loaded wheat and wool in Sydney, Conrad carried sacks aboard for a steady twelve hours daily, less time for meals. They had a stormy passage home, arriving in London after almost exactly a year, at the end of a passage which had taken 106 days.

This experience on the *Duke of Sutherland* was disillusioning to Conrad, who had begun to feel that his physical strength was unequal to such ordeals. In the hope of improving his lot, he signed on in the S.S. *Europa* for the Mediterranean, evidently thinking that the greater comfort of the crew's quarters and the Mediterranean climate might compensate for the dirt and noise of a steamship. If he had also hoped for a call at Marseilles, he was disappointed. The *Europa* visited only Italian ports; he had a quarrel with her captain who was, he wrote to Uncle Thaddeus, a madman; and he got back to London with a feverish cold and a cough, distinctly ill.

Discouraged, he began to play with the idea of giving up the sea, writing to his uncle of a scheme to go to Canada as secretary to a businessman with political ambitions and interests in Canadian railroads, who had probably been a passenger on the *Duke of Sutherland* or the *Europa*. Alter-

natively, he suggested going to America or Australia, whence
he thought he could trade with the East Indies. Uncle Thaddeus, with heavy responsibilities at home, cast cold water on
these projects, telling his nephew that since he was now a
sailor, he had better stick to his profession and work up.

Conrad, whose schemes were usually the result of desperation, rather than plans fully worked out, came around to
his uncle's view. He had written to M. Delestang for a recommendation, which had arrived, generously stating that
he had served with ships of the firm for three years, thus
giving the impression that he had spent more time at sea
than was the case. With his record on the *Mavis, Duke of
Sutherland,* and *Europa,* he was qualified as far as experience
went to sit for the London examination which would give
him the rank of junior officer. Several months of study
would be required, however, before he could master tech-
nical details and perfect his vocabulary in English. After
some hesitation, Conrad made up his mind to spend these
months ashore, helped by his allowance from Uncle Thaddeus. Too poor to live inside London, he found a cheap
room in Stoke Newington, and settled to work. He was
bitterly lonely, having nothing to do but study or make the
rounds of shipowners' offices in the City to fill out forms in
hope of a tolerable berth. He had no acquaintances in London, which was not an easy place in which to make them,
since most Englishmen did not frequent the commercial
section of the port. Despite stringent economy, money slipped
through his fingers. It was an unhappy time.

The examination for the rank of officer, held under the
auspices of the Marine Department of the Board of Trade,

was intended as a real test of a candidate's competency. An elderly examiner in seamanship took in the foreign-looking young man with the curious accent and, crossing his legs in a relaxed manner, began to ask questions in a mild voice. A couple of hours later, he was still asking without any apparent purpose of coming to an end. Conrad had entered the examination room certain that his knowledge was more than adequate, but queer ideas began to run through his head while he considered his answers. "This ancient person is so near his grave that he must have lost all notion of time. He is considering this examination in terms of eternity. It is all very well for him. His race is run. But I may find myself coming out of this room into the world of men a stranger, friendless, forgotten by my very landlady, even were I able after this endless experience to remember the way to my hired home." To be sure, such thoughts did not really pass through his mind in coherent form while the examiner was resolving his lingering doubts about the competence of this obvious foreigner; but he did feel the distraction of light-headed fantasies as two hours lengthened into three. Convinced, even if unwillingly, that the young man knew his job, the examiner fell silent at last, dipping his pen in the ink to write out the pass-slip, which he handed over without a word of congratulation, merely inclining his head in answer to a foreign-looking bow.

"Well, I thought you were never coming out," remarked the doorkeeper, as Conrad stopped to pick up his hat and tip him a shilling. He pulled out his watch and made it just under three hours. "I don't think this ever happened with any of the gentlemen before."

Successful, though squeezed like a lemon, the young man got himself outside before he had recovered sufficiently to measure his achievement. His foot was firmly on the ladder to success, and after two further examinations, he would be a captain! Uncle Thaddeus, writing in a spirit of heartfelt approval, dwelt on his hard work in the face of difficulties with the language and prejudice against a foreigner. His nephew had proved himself a true Bobrowski.

With only a brand-new certificate to offer, Conrad was lucky to find a berth as third officer two months later on one of the crack ships of the Australia run. The *Loch Etive* was a full-rigged iron clipper only three years old and just starting on her third trip to Australia. Her captain, William Stuart, had been a shipmaster since he was twenty and had been captain of the *Tweed* for fourteen years, during which he had piled up records for speed on the China run, on one occasion beating the mail steamer from Hong Kong to Singapore by a day and a half. Such a man was necessarily a driver; and it was Stuart's ambition to make similar records in the *Loch Etive,* though iron ships were not as fast as wooden ones. His chief mate, a youngish man and a good sailor, though hard of hearing, shared his ambition and would drive the *Loch Etive* with all sails set in worsening weather until Stuart himself would come up to remonstrate. The howling of the wind and the deafness of the mate gave rise to altercations, snatches of which were audible to Conrad as he waited for the order to shorten sail.

"By heavens, Mr. Purdue!" Stuart would yell. "I used to carry on sail in my time, but . . ." The rest would be carried away in a gust of wind.

"She seems to stand it very well," the mate would protest in the next lull.

"Any fool can carry sail on a ship — " screamed the captain.

The point of the row was that neither the mate nor the captain wanted to be the one to give the actual order which would slow the ship's pace, so that they would go on yelling at one another until both realized in some particularly alarming gust that they had to do something. In justice to Captain Stuart, it may be said that he died on the *Loch Etive* seventeen years later without ever having lost a mast or a man overboard. He seems to have known just how far he could go with a ship, which is a quality worth passing on to junior officers, even if his demonstrations were a little dangerous. Conrad, promoted to officer of the watch by the illness of the second mate, was caught on one occasion by a sudden shift of wind. The captain did not come on deck during the excitement that followed, but he sent for his third mate after the watch was over to demand an explanation. Why hadn't he seen the shift coming and had his courses hauled up, the captain wanted to know in ominous tones. Stuart had a capacity for finding fault in a manner which the culprit never forgot, but in this case his quick-witted third mate had taken his measure.

"Well, sir, she was going eleven knots very nicely, and I thought she would do for another half hour or so."

Eleven knots was a temptation, and the captain fell for it. "Ah yes, another half hour. That's the way ships get dismasted," he said, dismissing the subject with a mildness almost unprecedented. The mate went out, very carefully closing the door.

Conrad had a lot to learn from Captain Stuart. One morning, scarcely moving on a glassy sea, they caught sight of a derelict ship and, as they came a little nearer, realized that there were men aboard. She was dismasted and sinking. Clearly the efforts of the men at the pumps could not keep her afloat for long, while as yet the *Loch Etive* appeared to make no progress toward her in the gentle breeze. Captain Stuart yelled for a couple of boats to be lowered, and he took Conrad aside for a word of warning. "You look out as you come alongside that she doesn't take you down with her. You understand?"

"Heavens! As if in such an emergency one stopped to think of danger," said the young man to himself.

Captain Stuart picked up the unspoken protest. "What you are going for is to save life, not drown your boat's crew for nothing." Nor did he let the matter rest, but as they returned with the rescued seamen, he called down in the sarcastic tone which made him feared, rather than liked, "So you have brought the boat back after all, have you?"

Another memorable experience on the *Loch Etive* was Conrad's sight of his first whaler, the *Alaska,* two years out from New York and 215 days on the cruising ground. It was January, and the *Loch Etive* was on her way back. She dropped off a keg full of old Sydney newspapers and a couple of boxes of figs to mark the Christmas season, while the young man brooded over a life which kept one out of contact with shore entanglements for more than two years.

They were seven weeks in Sydney, left in January, and were back in London on April 23, 1881, after a passage of 103 days, slowed by bad weather. Conrad was paid off at the comparatively magnificent rate of three pounds ten shillings a month; and according to his usual habit, he did not rejoin. Though he was shaping into an excellent seaman, he was still only twenty-two, quickly bored by routine, and of the opinion that he was merely beginning to see the world. Why go to Australia again when the whole Far East remained unexplored? Besides, it was an object with him to have experience as a second mate as soon as possible, which might not be easy in the *Loch Etive*.

Several frustrating weeks were consumed in looking for a ship, during which Conrad's hard-earned money once more melted away, while the loneliness of London life oppressed him. In June, however, the 1236-ton sailing ship the *Annie Frost,* back from China after ten months, anchored briefly in the Downs off Deal, preparatory to unloading cargo in Le Havre. From there she would return to London in order to set out again with little delay. It seems to have been the practice for seamen in want of work to join such ships at the Downs if they could, instead of waiting to scramble for available berths when they reached London. Conrad apparently did this, for he was not entered in the ship's roster, as he must have been at the start of any new voyage. But as the *Annie Frost* was being towed out of Le Havre at night, she struck the quay wall and bridge, damaging her rails and starboard quarter. What happened to Conrad we do not precisely know, but the *Annie Frost* sailed without him, while Uncle Thaddeus wrote: "Thanks be to God you escaped, that you are active; that you have got off with only a few days' illness, and that your stay in the hospital has done you good — which rarely happens. I send you the ten pounds you asked for and I shall not deduct it from your allowance. I send it to you as a 'distressed seaman.' " So saying, Uncle Thaddeus entered the sum in a notebook in which he recorded his expenses for his nephew. If this seems a trifle ungenerous of him, we may also consider the fact that, since Conrad was not on the ship's roster, there is no proof that he was not making up another story to gull his uncle out of ten pounds. Perhaps the smallness of the sum makes it unlikely, but his record is against him in the matter.

Balked of adventure on the *Annie Frost,* Conrad was in a mood to get to the Far East by any method which did not involve eternal waiting in London. In consequence, he signed on as second mate aboard the 450-ton *Palestine* which was going up to Newcastle to load coal for Bangkok. The *Palestine* was a very old ship indeed and had been laid up in dock for a long while until her owner had recently scraped together money for this voyage. She was covered with London grime, her fittings were primitive, and nothing was new on her but the captain and crew. Captain Beard had been for many years in the coasting trade and then in the Mediterranean and West Indies. Though a good seaman, he had never been round the Horn or the Cape of Good Hope, those two passages which set the seal of experience on a captain. Both he and his first mate were aging men who had not made any great mark in their profession and must put up with a far too elderly ship on a long voyage and carrying a somewhat dangerous cargo. The new second mate, immensely proud of being a real watch-keeping officer for the first time, was twenty-three.

They started out from London with sand ballast to pick up their coal in Newcastle, only to run into a gale which stuck in the memory of coastal shipping for years as *the* October gale. Naturally they were blown off course, bulwarks were smashed and decks were flooded; but the worst of it was that the ballast shifted, forcing them to go below and try to right it. "There we were in that vast hold, gloomy like a cavern, the tallow dips stuck and flickering on the beams, the gale howling above, the ship tossing about like mad on her side; there we all were . . . hardly able to keep our feet . . . trying to toss shovelfuls of wet sand up to windward. At every tumble of the ship you could see vaguely in the dim light men falling down with a great flourish of shovels."

After the gale died out, they were picked up by a tug and brought into Newcastle, where they found they had missed their turn for lading and had to wait a month. Eventually they got their coal aboard and were prepared to set out, the three officers, eight able seamen, and two boys. At this moment, they had a collision at the entrance to the port with an incoming steamer, resulting in damage which delayed them another three weeks.

In January, by now three months out of London, they started out in beautiful winter weather for Bangkok. This lasted until they were three hundred miles into the Atlantic when a storm blew up. "Day after day and night after night there was nothing around the ship but the howl of the wind, the tumult of the sea, the noise of the water pouring over her deck . . . She tossed, she pitched, she stood on her head, she sat on her tail, she rolled, she groaned, and we had to hold on while on deck and cling to our bunks when below in a constant effort of body and worry of mind."

The ship was working her timbers loose and began to leak badly, "not enough to drown us at once, but enough to kill us with the work at the pumps . . . we pumped watch and watch for dear life; and it seemed to last for months, for years, for all eternity, as though we had been dead and gone to a hell for sailors . . . The sails blew away . . . the ocean poured over her, and we did not care . . . As soon as we had crawled on deck I used to take a round turn with a rope about the men, the pumps, and the mainmast, and we turned, we turned incessantly with the water to our waists, to our necks, over our heads. It was all one. We had forgotten how it felt to be dry."

Eventually the gale died, but the crew had no heart to go on. The boats were gone, the decks swept clean, men's sea trunks splintered and washed away, the cabin guttered, and the stores spoiled. The ship still leaked, and they had to pump their way back to Falmouth in the teeth of a wind which had veered east into precisely the opposite direction.

There was plenty to repair in Falmouth, and it took time. Some of the coal had to be unloaded to caulk leaks. The crew, which had had enough of the *Palestine,* departed, leaving only the elderly officers, who could hope for nothing better, and the young second mate, who wanted to get to Bangkok. Uncle Thaddeus, alarmed by this fresh outburst of the Korzeniowski temperament, wrote with some eloquence: "Your cool judgment seems to have deserted you in accepting such a wretched ship as the *Palestine.* I quite understand that you made up your mind to do so to avoid being a burden to me on land, and to qualify by serving as a second officer for your final exam . . . But if you succeed in drowning yourself, it won't profit you to arrive at the Valley of Jehoshaphat in the rank of a third or second officer! . . . Danger is certainly part of a sailor's life, but that does not preclude you from having a sensible attachment to life . . . Think well over, my dear fellow, what you ought to do. I shall not come down on you if you go back to land, and I shall try to help you . . . I do not want for the sake of saving three to five hundred roubles to see you at the bottom of the sea, or ill or injured, or crippled with rheumatism for the rest of your life."

All the same, they hired a fresh crew and started off, only to be back in a week with what amounted to a mutiny on their hands, the crew refusing to start for Bangkok in a ship that still required pumping for eight hours a day in any weather. They did a few more repairs while the owner, short of money, came down from London for the day and said she was "right as a little fiddle." She tried to start out with a third crew but leaked worse than ever. Even Conrad, who had been whiling away his time by reading Shakespeare in a cheap one-volume edition, took a break to dash up to London where he went to a music hall, lunched and dined in a "swell place in Regent Street" and bought himself a set of Byron and a rug. Pay being what it was, this mild dissipation consumed his entire earnings from the *Palestine* thus far, well over six months.

By this time, the *Palestine* was in the hands of brokers, who were willing to put in cash to protect their investment. The cargo was completely unloaded. The ship went into drydock to be recaulked and recoppered. The *Palestine* had acquired such a bad reputation that no crew could be found on the south coast. Men were sent down from Liverpool, and once more the voyage started.

She was not a speedy ship, but she lumbered into the Indian Ocean eventually, setting her course for Java Head. It was Conrad, going casually below to get the men an extra bucket of water out of the spare tank for washing their clothes, who noticed the horrible smell of paraffin and smoke. Investigation confirmed his guess. The cargo was on fire. Broken up into powder by the loading and unloading, and thoroughly wetted down because these operations had been performed in the pouring rain, then finally shut into an enclosed space in temperatures which steadily rose as they lumbered across southern seas, the coal had ignited.

The captain decided to go on to Bangkok, rather than making for western Australia, which was nearer. He hoped that if they battened down everything, they might stifle the fire aboard for lack of air. They tried; but the old *Palestine* leaked out of a thousand tiny crevices topside, however tight she might be below the waterline. Air got in, and coils of poisonous smoke came oozing out. They tried water, pumping as constantly to get water inside as they once had done to get it out; but still the *Palestine* moved over the almost flat sea in a mist of smoke. They tried digging down to the fire, but had to abandon the effort since nobody could endure conditions below for more than a minute. They put the longboat into the water and had the others ready in case they needed to abandon ship; but suddenly the smoke began to decrease as they went on pouring in water, so that less than two hundred miles from Java Head, the fire seemed out. Everyone went about with broad grins; the men washed their clothes and had a special dinner to celebrate. The ship crawled on.

At ten o'clock the following morning while Conrad was casually chatting with the carpenter by the mainmast, the deck blew up. When he picked himself up, dazed, his hair, eyebrows, mustache and beard were burned off. His face was black, his shirt in rags, his cheek laid open. Everyone in the crew was hurt, but none disabled. The deck was a tangle of planks, and from the wreckage arose a whitish, greasy-looking smoke. The masts were still standing, but no one could tell how far they had been burned through below or in which direction they would eventually fall. A steamer came by bound for Batavia and took them in tow, on the general understanding that the *Palestine* could be scuttled in shallow water to put out the fire, after which she could be pumped dry again and continue her journey.

They went a little faster under tow, so that the movement fanned the flames. After dark that night they saw red fire for the first time, got their things together, cut the tow, and put the boats out. The steamer, which had mail for Singapore and was in a hurry, offered to take them to that port; but the skipper decided they were not too far off land to get there on their own. There were three boats, one for each of the officers; and Captain Beard said that they must keep together. For this reason, they did not make a start till dawn, but drifted around the burning ship, on which the flames leaped high, surmounted by black smoke pouring up into the sky. At daylight, when there was little left but a charred shell, they got out the oars. As they passed her, the *Palestine* went down head first in a hiss of steam.

Conrad's boat, which was the smallest, had no sail; but he rigged one out of a boat awning and a spare oar, with a boathook for a yard. She was overmasted, he admits, but in a fair wind she outran the others. In this way, therefore, in command of his own boat, Conrad arrived in the Far East at one of those semiderelict ports which are not in themselves the least romantic. Yet, "a puff of wind," he says, " ... laden with strange odors [came] out of the still night — the first sigh of the East."

The tale of the *Palestine*, shaped years later by Conrad into "Youth," puts this narrative into the mouth of a middle-aged adventurer able to look back on the young second mate, to find him absurd, even foolish, and yet filled with an unextinguishable ardor which is also reflected in the ancient ship on whose stern was painted the motto DO OR DIE. The details of the voyage in "Youth" follow closely the actual course of events; but even more carefully do they bring out the quality of this young man who roamed the world in a spirit of adventure, rootless, uncertain of any ultimate purpose, driven to match his puny strength against the force of wind and weather, eager for novelty and bored by routine. Conrad's nostalgia for the boy that he had been is as clearly reflected as his sense of youthful folly or his knowledge that the spirit of adventure can be retained by simpler people for their entire lives, but not by him. Though he regrets the passing of it from himself, he knows that wisdom has caused the change in him as much as age.

5

Captain Korzeniowski

THE VOYAGE of the *Palestine* represents, both in Conrad's life and in his fiction, the romantic boy who had made up his mind in childhood to become one of the explorers of the earth. In fact, however, Conrad was already developing into someone far more complex. In 1883, Thaddeus, who met him for the first time since Marseilles at a German spa where he had gone to take the waters, was aware that his nephew had grown up. In the last five years Conrad had overcome the handicaps of his foreign extraction and had established himself in the British merchant marine with every prospect of becoming a captain before he was thirty. It was a remarkable achievement, and one due to a combination of hard work and ability, which Uncle Thaddeus once more hailed as true Bobrowski traits. Recognizing Conrad's maturity, Bobrowski handed over about three hundred pounds which had accumulated for his nephew through various legacies and which Conrad intended to invest in a transport firm called Barr, Moering and Company, on the advice of Adolf Krieger, an old friend from Marseilles who had come to London and found himself a job in the firm. Furthermore, Thaddeus agreed to continue the allowance until Conrad was a captain and fully able to look after himself. Meanwhile, he continued to mark every small expenditure on his nephew in his account book.

Bobrowski's account book and the critical tone of many of his letters have encouraged some people to suppose that Conrad secretly resented Thaddeus, but evidence suggests that the bond between them was a strong one. Conrad writes with pleasure of reunion with the uncle who was the chief link with his boyhood, portraying Bobrowski as expressing his affection far more spontaneously in words than he usually did by letter.

Continuing to show the marked abilities that his uncle admired, Conrad passed his examination for first mate in this same year of 1883. This time he drew a different examiner, who put him on an imaginary ship under certain weather conditions and told him to execute a complex maneuver. Before they were halfway through, he did some damage to the ship. Directly Conrad had grappled with this emergency, he presented another. A moment later, he placed a second ship in front of him in a dangerous position.

"I should have seen that ship before," the candidate protested.

"No, you couldn't. The weather's thick."

While collision was being staved off, the examiner was ready with another crisis. Eventually, after a long and hideous passage in the unluckiest ship of all time, Conrad found

Joseph Conrad at twenty-six

himself off a lee shore with outlying sandbanks. He hesitated.

"Well?"

"I will have to think a little, sir."

"Doesn't look as if there were much time to think."

"No, sir," the candidate retorted, goaded, "not on board a ship I could see. But so many accidents have happened that I really can't remember what there's left for me to work with."

"You've done very well, so far," the examiner conceded grudgingly. His mind was soon made up; and after a grilling of no more than forty minutes, Conrad was handed the precious certificate, announcing his competence to hold a first officer's job if he could get one. Berths being hard to find, Conrad never actually served as first mate until after he had gained his captain's certificate three years later.

Meanwhile, the development of Conrad's temperament showed itself in other ways, which Uncle Thaddeus might have attributed to the Korzeniowskis. In September 1883, for instance, Conrad sailed on the *Riversdale,* a Liverpool ship with a general cargo bound for South Africa, India, the Far East, and hence around the world. His part in this venture, however, ended four months later in Madras, where he left after a quarrel with her captain. Conrad was always thin-skinned, but in this instance he may possibly have been in the right, seeing that six weeks later Captain McDonald grounded the *Riversdale* two hundred miles further up the Indian coast and was relieved of his command.

Quitting the *Riversdale* with the modest sum of twenty-four pounds due him in wages, Conrad lost no time in making for Bombay, where he would have a better chance of finding another berth. A week or so later, as he was sitting on the verandah of the Sailors' Home in Bombay, he saw a lovely ship looking almost like a private yacht glide into the harbor. She was a full-rigged iron sailing ship called the *Narcissus,* trading between British ports and Bombay and, as it proved, in want of a replacement for her second officer. Conrad joined her at the end of April and left her at Dunkirk in mid-October, after a voyage which might be described as not untypical. The *Narcissus* had sailed from Bombay with twenty-four officers and men, including an American Negro called Joseph Barron, who died on the voyage "after an awful gale in the vicinity of the Needles."

A death at sea had an unsettling effect on any crew, while that of the *Narcissus*, which was drawn from ten different nations, was unusually restless. On the way out from England, the ship had replaced five men in Capetown and six more in Bombay, as well as an officer. In the memory of any commonplace seaman, however, the voyage of the *Narcissus* might have been passed over as unremarkable, including its inevitable gale and the death of the Negro. Nevertheless, out of this experience Conrad fashioned a novel called *The Nigger of the Narcissus*, which was written many years later, expressing much of his thought on life at sea, death, moral values, and human nature. This is a very different story from "Youth," lacking its simplicity and faithfulness to actual events, which are enlarged and deepened by incidents taken from elsewhere.

An example of this may be seen in the death of the Negro, which was paralleled by another death on Conrad's very next voyage. In April 1885, he sailed as second mate on the *Tilkhurst,* bound for Singapore with a cargo of coal which, there, had to be unloaded onto small native boats, a clumsy operation which took a month. During this period one of the seamen, William Cummings, was hit on the head in a drunken quarrel. At the time he seemed none the worse, but as the ship moved up the Malacca Straits, he complained of headaches and presently had bouts of delirium. He was kept below, his mates looking after him with an anxiety which was increased because the light winds of the straits offered no crisis to distract their attention. Despite their vigilance, Cummings got out of his bed one night, eluded the watch, and jumped overboard. The ship, cursed by the suicide, as the men supposed, had a tedious passage of thirty-three days to Calcutta, where one of the seamen insisted on quitting. The strength of the superstition was the more remarkable because this particular man was too old to find another berth with any ease.

The thoughtful mood in which such incidents were woven into *The Nigger of the Narcissus* reveals a Conrad very different from the exuberant hero of "Youth." We must not read too much into fiction written so long after the event, but other evidence goes to show that by his late twenties Conrad had changed from the eager boy who had spent a gay time in Marseilles. It happened that while the *Tilkhurst* was loading coal for Singapore at Cardiff, Conrad had made the acquaintance of a Polish watchmaker in the town who had introduced him to his whole family. The son of the house, Spiridion, an intelligent young man of Conrad's age, soon became a close friend. During the *Tilkhurst*'s voyage, the two young Poles corresponded about the political state of affairs in England and Europe and their possible bearing on the future of Poland. To Poland's fate, Conrad wrote that he was despairingly indifferent, foreseeing that whatever changes there were in view for living nations, there was no hope of salvation for the dead. The tragedy of their country, he added, made personal happiness impossible for Poles, though in a friendly land they might find relative contentment.

This gloomy conclusion serves to remind us that Conrad had so far made contacts in England, rather than friends. There were one or two people he saw between voyages, but his actual shipmates drifted away and were lost. Captain Blake of the *Tilkhurst* was the only officer who ever invited him to visit his home, but Blake at the time was a dying man. Meanwhile, Conrad's natural restlessness was increased by the approach of his examination for captain, which he passed in October 1886, with flying colors. As he had perceived in advance, success brought him to the top of his profession, leaving him with nothing tangible to strive for.

What should he do with his captain's certificate? Discounting his ten weeks of coastal trade in the *Skimmer of the Seas*, Conrad had not made two voyages in the same ship since his arrival in England. Routine bored him, and in later life he would complain to his friends that most of a sailor's life was very dull. He had no desire to settle down in command of a ship making regular runs; indeed the prospect frightened him into a series of plans for escape.

The captain of the *Narcissus* had formerly been a whaler and still had hankerings after the big profits of a successful voyage, even though he had quit the trade for the sake of an easier climate. Conrad proposed a partnership, writing to Spiridion from the *Tilkhurst* that he planned to finance the enterprise by taking out life insurance which he could use as security for borrowing fifteen hundred pounds. He would have to pay interest on the loan as well as premiums on the insurance, but he intended to do this out of his allowance from Thaddeus and the earnings of his little fortune of three hundred pounds, now invested with Barr, Moering and

Company. Wondering briefly whether it made sense to go into whaling with money so expensively borrowed, he insisted to Spiridion that he was tired of low pay and lack of consideration from his employers. If he could make a bare living out of the sea by working for himself, he would be happy.

Spiridion poured cold water on this scheme, so typical of Conrad, to whom grass always looked greener on the other side of the fence. Whaling was abandoned; but even after the return of the *Tilkhurst* the new-made Captain Korzeniowski was discussing with his uncle a plan for working up Polish connections for Barr, Moering and Company, dreaming of a business career. He suggested another meeting with Bobrowski and had at last taken steps to be naturalized in England. Before he dared enter Russia, however, he needed a formal consent to his change of citizenship. Russian bureaucracy moved slowly; and in the meantime Conrad's Uncle Casimir died, leaving six children dependent on Thaddeus, who wrote that he could not afford to travel. Perhaps for this reason, the Barr, Moering scheme came to nothing, while Captain Korzeniowski branched out in a new direction. A London magazine called *Tit-Bits* was running a short-story contest, and Conrad tried his hand at an entry. "The Black Mate," a comedy about a mate gone prematurely gray, whose bottle of hair dye was broken in a storm at sea, was quite unsuited to the brooding intensity of Conrad's mind. It failed of its purpose and aroused no ambition in him to try again.

Finding it impossible to change his profession while his resources were so meager, Conrad soon accepted a job as first mate on the *Highland Forest*, which was tied up in Amsterdam during January 1887, waiting for a cargo for Java. Europe was in the grip of a cold wave which had frozen the Dutch canals, forcing goods for Amsterdam to pile up inland. Since the *Highland Forest* was temporarily without a captain, Conrad found himself in charge and, anxious to satisfy the owners, spent a good deal of his waking time in the warmly heated office of Hudig, the shipping agent, trying in vain to set a date for the cargo's arrival. Hudig would offer a cigar and the comfortable opinion that the owners would soon appoint their young first mate as captain. As time went by, ice melted, traffic jams were sorted out, and the *Highland Forest* began to take on cargo, it looked more and more as though Hudig might be right. Great was Conrad's disappointment when John MacWhirr, a stocky Irishman who had served two terms as mate on the *Highland Forest*, turned up to take command. He nodded grimly at Conrad's account of her stowage, which he had worked out according to prevailing textbook methods, remarking that it looked as though they would have a lively voyage.

They sailed for Java in mid-February and had an exceptionally stormy passage, during which the *Highland Forest* rolled like a ship possessed. Captain MacWhirr did not cease to remind his young first mate that he was responsible for not having understood the distribution of weights which the ship needed. Disappointed in his hopes and wounded in his pride of seamanship, Conrad was in a mood to think it no more than justice when he was hit on the back by a falling spar and sent sliding clear across the deck face down. Intense pain and partial paralysis followed, suggesting either a nerve injury or a psychological shock. While Conrad lay below enduring spasms of agony which made him question the point of living at all, the *Highland Forest* went through her worst week of tempest, causing even the stolid MacWhirr to exclaim afterward, "Man! It's a pairfect meeracle to me how she lived through it." In the intervals of freedom from pain, Conrad felt, and blamed himself for feeling, the sheer relief of not having to face those endless nights and days of struggle with the elements. His depression was deepened by experiencing the sensations of a malingerer against his will.

He was carried ashore in Singapore, where a doctor prescribed a three-months' rest in hospital. Used though Conrad was to periods of waiting between voyages, he found this disablement very hard to bear. As soon as he could walk without a stick, he made his way to the Officers' Sailors' Home in Singapore to inquire about a way to get back to England; but nothing offered. The seamen he met in this place fell into two groups. The born adventurers, in whose company he might normally have belonged, lived in a maze of plans, hopes, or dangers encountered in obscure corners of the sea. Still walking with a limp, however, and struggling with one of the bouts of depression which were becoming as normal to him as fits of romantic exaltation, Conrad naturally gravitated toward the men who had been stranded in the East by accident and had stayed because they found conditions easy. They were men who loved short passages, deck chairs, large native crews, and the distinction of being white. Their conversation turned on strokes of luck in finding soft billets where a man could get along without doing much work.

In such a mood, Conrad put aside his prejudice against steamships, signing on as first mate in the S.S. *Vidar*, which was in the Borneo coastal trade, part-owned by Craig, its captain, and part by an Arab potentate descended from Mohammed. There were four white men aboard the *Vidar*, the captain and first mate with two engineers. She carried in addition a native boatswain, eleven Malay seamen, and eighty-two Chinese coolies for loading and unloading. She took out a cargo of general supplies, returning chiefly with rattan and gutta-percha, which were brought down to river landings in native canoes.

The voyages of the *Vidar*, which took about three and a half weeks each, brought Conrad for the first time into intimate contact with the life of the East. As he noted himself later on, the sailor is in some ways the least traveled of mankind because he takes his house and community with him wherever he goes. Furthermore, the big ports which engaged in foreign trade were meeting grounds for many peoples and divided into racial quarters where like lived with like. On the *Vidar*, Conrad, picking up Malay with the speed of a born linguist, made acquaintance with the tiny settlements of Borneo and the Celebes.

Typical of the *Vidar*'s ports of call was the Berouw River on the east coast of Borneo, its mouth so swampy with the silt carried down from inland and so tangled with mangroves that it presented an apparently impenetrable screen of tropical vegetation, though which it oozed, rather than flowed, into the sea. Once past this maze of dead-end inlets and shifting sandbanks, the *Vidar* chugged its way up a muddy river running between solid walls of jungle so interlaced with creepers that its twenty-foot snakes or fabulous orchids lived in a green gloom. Huge crocodiles sunned themselves on sandbanks, but the chatter of monkeys and other jungle sounds were literally stifled by the matted growth of the forest. It was breathlessly hot, cooled in the evenings by tropical downpours which dropped as much as five inches of rain at a time. The jungle steamed and was obscured every morning in a foggy cloud.

The *Vidar* went over thirty miles up the Berouw, past the trading settlement of Samburakat to another place five miles further upstream called Berouw or Patusan, where a Scottish trader named Tom Lingard had built a station and a wharf some thirty years back. Patusan consisted of a quarter of a mile of palm-leaf huts built out into the river on stilts and connected by a footpath running behind them which was in turn backed by the impenetrable jungle.

Originally infested by Malay pirates who preyed indifferently on their own kind and foreign adventurers, the Berouw River had for a long time been a monopoly of Lingard's because no one else knew how to navigate the entrance. Lingard was a man with an interest in native life who had looked on himself as father and protector of the people on his river. In return, they had christened him the Rajah Laut, or King of the Sea, in gratitude for his victories over the pirates. The Rajah Laut was a short, jovial man, by now growing old, who was often to be seen in Singapore, the more so as much of his business was now entrusted to his nephews James and Joshua. "His thunderous laughter filled the verandah," says Conrad in a famous passage, "rolled over the hotel garden, overflowed into the street . . . In the big billiard room perspiring men in their cotton singlets would stop their game, listen, cue in hand, for a while through the open windows, then nod their moist faces at each other sagaciously and whisper, 'The old fellow is talking about his river.'"

Perhaps he was, but by the time of Conrad's employment on the *Vidar*, Arab traders had learned the secret of the entrance, while a power struggle between two inland rajahs extending downriver to Patusan had once more thrown the area into chaos. Nevertheless, four white men still lived there, clinging precariously to their domain, which consisted of a couple of large, decaying houses with wide verandahs, a rickety dock protruding from one of these, and an abandoned hulk which was used for storage.

The strongest personality among the white men on the Berouw was James Lingard, Tom's nephew, a six-foot, youngish man with a swaggering air and dressed, at least in Singapore, in business suit and jeweled watch chain. James Lingard made several visits to Singapore in the *Vidar*, whose crew nicknamed him Tuan Jim, or Lord Jim, on account of his lofty manner.

Jim Lingard, who had business connections in Singapore and was both young and energetic, made a strange contrast to Charles Olmeijer, a relative of Tom Lingard's wife and his original agent on the Berouw. An ineffective man, who had long ceased to struggle with trade competitors or the enervating tropical climate, Olmeijer, called Almayer by the Englishmen on the *Vidar*, kept up his dignity by an absurd pretentiousness. His house, which the crew of the *Vidar* referred to as "Almayer's folly," was an elaborate structure commenced in anticipation of trade expansion which never occurred, and beginning to fall to bits before it was completed. He kept a flock of white geese, the only ones on that coast, and presented a goose to the *Vidar* with the air of an eastern potentate bestowing largesse. In Conrad's day, the *Vidar* had to take him out a pony, though the little track behind the houses of the village was the only place where he could ride it. Almayer made no secret of the fact that he was too good for a world that had treated him badly, bolstering up his ego by mysterious hopes of discovering gold up the river, down which gold objects occasionally made their way in native canoes. He had no serious intention of undertaking an exploration, but tried to establish relations with the inland tribes by importing them forbidden arms in the *Vidar*.

So out of touch with reality was Almayer that the men of the *Vidar* made a joke of him. To Conrad, however, he had an especial fascination, possibly because his early life had been spent in just such a dream world. Apollo Korzeniowski, exiled to a settlement which was equally remote, looked down on the natives and, keeping to himself, taught his son to sign himself, "Pole, Catholic, gentleman" with a disregard of actual circumstances which was as complete as that of Almayer. One needed only to substitute dreams of Polish freedom for Almayer's fantasies of hidden gold. Whether for this reason or for some other, the figure of Almayer haunted Conrad's imagination for years.

There were two more white men in Patusan, both derelicts, one Russian and the other Dutch. In addition there was a Chinese trader, whose daughter was married to Jim Lingard and who kept what might be described as the local bar. Among the scattered native groups which dotted the river, as developments dot a modern highway, was a stockaded village of Bugis, or native Malay traders, whose chieftain, "Captain" Dain, was a particular friend of Captain Craig's and his principal exporter.

The Berouw River was not the only port of call of the *Vidar*, but it was the most remote and, being connected with the hinterland by its great river highway, one of the most profitable for trade. The *Vidar*, which often had to wait for expected cargo, and being without winches used coolie labor for the loading, would usually spend several days at Patusan. The strangeness of the place, narrowed by the jungle, yet connected with unexplored distances by its river highway, made an immense impression on Conrad's mind. He talked Malay to the natives, learned some of their customs, respected Dain, despised the local rajah, and learned by heart the landmarks of the river. All this had its fascination, but life moved slowly in that climate, while most of what the *Vidar* did was mere routine. Craig thought he had found the best chief officer he ever had, but Conrad's active temperament was soon fretted by having no fresh challenges to meet. His limp was getting better, but his eyes began giving trouble and he worried nervously about going blind. In later life he wore a monocle, a fashion in those days instead of bifocals, which allowed him to scan print with one eye and glare belligerently across the room with the other. Very possibly it was aboard the *Vidar* he began to feel the need of this arrangement.

All in all, it would be impossible to say that Conrad was

happy on the *Vidar*, though Captain Craig perceived nothing wrong, merely remarking that his mate spent a good deal of time scribbling notes in his cabin, all of which have vanished without trace. No one could have been more surprised than Craig when after eighteen months of satisfactory service his mate, who had liked him, liked his engineers, learned Malay, and taken interest in every place and personality on the *Vidar*'s route, announced one day, when they got back to Singapore, that he was leaving. The captain hoped he would find what he was looking for; the second engineer supposed he was going home to marry some silly girl; the first engineer put the whole thing down to liver trouble and offered to buy him two bottles of patent medicine out of his own pocket. Or so Conrad says.

Even this handsome offer did no good. It seemed to Conrad that he had been marking time and going soft, that he ought to get out of the coastal trade, go back to England, and face the challenge of the mighty oceans. He could hardly wait to get started, and only the fact that no home-bound mail boat was due for three or four days directed his steps toward the Officers' Sailors' Home instead of the ticket office. He got there before lunch, more or less at the same time that the harbormaster sent down a note to the steward there about an Australian ship called the *Otago*, which was stranded in Bangkok without a captain and needed one at once. Craig's recommendation and Conrad's own experience in sailing ships pointed to him as the man for the emergency. Naturally he leaped at his first chance of command, and by ten o'clock that same night he was on his way to Bangkok.

His chance had come at last, and his spirits soared. No

matter that the *Otago*'s former captain had died and that
for some reason the owners seemed inaccessible by cable.
She was his own, and he liked the look of her when first
he laid his eyes on her high-bred lines. His meeting with
Born, the first mate, however, soon gave him a hint that
trouble lay ahead. Captain Snadden had sailed from Newcastle, Australia, in August 1887. He had discharged coal in
Haiphong, French Indochina, and had kept the ship idle for
three weeks in that hot, unhealthy port. Apparently he was
already ill and mentally confused, though Born said he also
was having an affair with a woman in the town. At all
events he left Haiphong without proper cargo or ballast, intending to beat up to Hong Kong, right in the teeth of the
prevailing monsoon. Leaving this hopeless task to his mate,
he retired to his cabin, where he solaced himself for long
hours by playing the violin. Eventually, sick and overcome
by the sheer impossibility of making Hong Kong without
adequate food or water, he consented to turn south, but died
in the South China Sea at the entrance to the Gulf of Siam.

Mr. Born, now left in charge, had the choice of making
for Singapore or Bangkok. He chose the latter because he
wanted to be appointed captain, though he did not have
a master's certificate. In Singapore, there would always be
somebody qualified for the job, whereas Bangkok was a
Siamese town with no place for an unemployed captain to
linger. Unfortunately for these plans, the harbormaster in
Bangkok lost no time in cabling to Singapore, as a result
of which Conrad appeared in about four days. Disappointed,
Born especially resented his new captain's youth and lack
of experience.

Conrad's poor relations with his first mate added unwelcome complications to a host of troubles which he found waiting for him. Captain Snadden, it turned out, had not communicated with the owners in Adelaide since leaving Australia about eight months earlier. Not unnaturally they wanted to know what the *Otago* had done with her cargo, whether she had taken on more, if so, where it had been landed, and in particular what moneys were due to them. No clear records existed; but it soon appeared that the captain had sold everything movable for cash, so that Conrad had to raise money for buying rope and sailcloth as well as replenishing stores. Furthermore, the late captain had owned a share in the *Otago,* which his executors wanted to turn into cash for his widow.

Bangkok in the hot, wet monsoon season proved no healthier than Haiphong. Twenty miles upriver from the Bight of Bangkok, the town was a completely eastern city, the front part of which was literally afloat. For nearly four miles along the riverbank, houses built on rafts were moored eight or ten deep in a picturesque huddle broken only by narrow waterways for getting about. What remained of the river was crowded with sailing junks or cargo boats of gondola shape with rounded tops of basketwork, each housing a family which made its living out of water transport. Sanitation was unknown, while flies and mosquitoes abounded. Conrad was urged to leave the river for the open sea, but could not budge without supplies and cargo. Presently his steward was sent to a hospital ashore with cholera. The Chinese replacement ran away three days later with Conrad's modest reserve of cash, saved from his pay on the *Vidar*. Next, Born was carried to hospital with fever. He had made no secret of his enmity to Conrad, but, having a wife and child in Sydney, he begged most piteously not to be left behind. In vain did the doctor warn that he would be of little use on the voyage and might not even survive it. Since the second officer was the stupidest man Conrad ever met during his life at sea, it would have been only prudent to replace Born; but Conrad could not bring himself to do it. Born was carried aboard when they left, while the doctor certified that cholera, dysentery, and malaria had appeared among the crew.

Conrad had been lucky enough to secure a cargo of teak, but the loading had taken sixteen days. The crew of the *Otago* endured this ordeal fairly well, most men improving in health and being able to move about the decks, but all sighing for the fresh breezes of the open sea to end their troubles. Unfortunately, the Gulf of Siam can be hot and airless, so that they moved out into a dead calm.

Almost immediately two men came down with fever, and Conrad went to the medicine chest for quinine. There were five large bottles of the powdered sort, one two-thirds empty and the others sealed in their original wrappings. On top of them lay a letter from the doctor, warning that he felt sure there would be a recurrence of the diseases with which they had left the port. He was right. Day after day they drifted helplessly, now moving with some current, now for a moment fanned by the whisper of a breeze. Meanwhile sickness ran through the ship, conditions fluctuating from day to day so that nobody was permanently bedridden; but none was fit for work and all depended on the precious bottles of quinine.

Pretty soon the first container was empty. Conrad reached for another and undid the wrapper, only to find that Captain Snadden had sold the medicine in Haiphong, replacing it with an inexpensive powder to cover up his theft.

The loss of the quinine made all the difference to that nightmare of a voyage. Only two people were unaffected by fever, Conrad himself and the cook, a pleasant, imperturbable man in his forties with a damaged heart, who moved with caution and could not exert himself much. Conrad did his best, managing to get the *Otago* about a hundred and fifty miles downcoast, where he maneuvered desperately close to shore in hopes of a land breeze, attracting the attention of Chinese pirates and losing once and for all the respect of Born, who was by now able to stagger on deck and appreciate his captain's recklessness.

For seventeen days Conrad was continuously on deck. When wind finally rose and it was necessary to spread sail, he led his stumbling men from one rope to another, while the cook, though forbidden to lift weights, hauled with the rest. They came into Singapore with a forecastle full of men who had to be carried ashore, with Born steering, propped in place by coils of rope, and Conrad coping with the anchors single-handed, while he and the cook rushed around to loosen sheets and halyards, so that the ship would lose her way before ramming something.

"The Shadow Line," in which Conrad recounts these experiences, is like "Youth" a piece of fiction. Also like "Youth," it seems to keep fairly closely to the actual events, which can be confirmed here and there by other authorities. If occasionally its incidents are embroidered, it remains a story which illustrates Conrad's abilities, but also his profound self-distrust. He blamed himself, he says, for the whole tragedy because he had never thought to unwrap those medicine bottles and inspect them in Bangkok. The voyage had made him used to being captain, but his nerves were constantly on the stretch because he demanded perfection of himself.

"You must be jolly tired by this time," commented an elderly captain who had been instrumental in getting him the job on the *Otago*.

"No," he said. "Not tired. But I'll tell you how I feel. I feel old."

The captain admitted he looked older, but advised him not to make too much of things, either good or bad.

"Life at half-speed," Conrad retorted. "Not everybody can do that."

The old captain's advice was sound, but Conrad, sailing for Australia with a fresh crew and the unavoidable Born, could not take it. It is true that as he recovered his strength, Born proved himself a good seaman, but he never quite trusted his captain's judgment. Inclined to take responsibility hard, Conrad might have been better served by a man who admired him.

Henry Simpson and Sons, of Adelaide, owners of the *Otago,* were more appreciative, though apparently their experience of trade with the Far East had given them a dislike of risks for the moment. Conrad spent a few months in coastal trade, reluctantly moving between Sydney, Melbourne, and Port Adelaide. It was with a sense of relief that he started loading a cargo for Mauritius in the French West Indies.

Coming out of a shipping office in Sydney, he ran into his old chief officer in the *Duke of Sutherland*, aboard which he had acted as night watchman for five long months while they waited for wool in Sydney. It had been one of his duties to help Mr. Baker up the gangway, for the mate, an excellent seaman afloat, was an alcoholic ashore. At that time Conrad had been a common seaman; now he was a captain and Baker was looking for a job. "His jet-black, curly hair had turned iron grey," says Conrad. "He was scrupulously neat as ever but frightfully threadbare. His shiny boots were worn down at heel." Conrad asked him to dinner and took him in a cab to see the *Otago;* but even though he discovered that Baker had given up liquor, he did not dare to admit that the *Otago*'s second mate was leaving to get married. "I could not have given orders to Mr. Baker — and I am sure he would not have taken them from me for very long." The captain who lacked self-confidence watched the burly, bull-necked figure walking away up the street, wondering whether his old officer had much more than the price of a night's lodging in his pocket. He had an impulse to call out after him, but told himself that even had he done so, Baker would never have turned back or taken the job.

The owners of the *Otago* had more faith in their young captain than he did in himself. Incorrigibly adventurous, he wanted to pass through the Torres Strait, admittedly a short-cut, but dangerous enough to require a rise in insurance premiums. To his astonishment, he received permission, "provided the season is not too far advanced to endanger the success of your passage." The season was advanced, but he went ahead, not without a slight qualm of conscience, and came through the straits in fine style, delighted to be in the seas first explored by Captain Cook, one of his boyhood heroes. He took a bearing on Persuasion Island, where Cook had landed for half an hour in 1762, imagining the lonely figure in three-cornered hat and square-skirted, laced coat pacing the rocky shore while his ship's boat lay off on her oars. Mr. Born, unsusceptible to such emotions, continued to regard his adventurous captain with foreboding.

They went to Mauritius for a cargo of sugar and were delayed there for eight weeks because a warehouse fire had consumed the local supply of sugar bags. The old French families of the place, impoverished but dignified, found Conrad a change from other shipmasters who were to be seen strolling the harbor in plain white ducks and sailor's caps, their fingernails black with tar. Captain Korzeniowski, nicknamed by his colleagues the Russian Count, was very much the dandy in dark coat, light vest and trousers, gloves and gold-headed cane, his head crowned by a black or gray derby, slightly tilted. He spoke French perfectly, and his conversation was that of a widely read and fascinating man. The Renouf family, consisting of two brothers and two unmarried sisters, all living with an elder married sister, found him attractive. The girls were pretty, bilingual, and flirtatious. Twenty-six-year-old Eugénie had an "Album de Confidences," in which she asked Conrad to answer personal questions such as, "Do you prefer blondes or brunettes?" or

"What is your favorite flower?" or "What natural gift would you most like to have had?" to which last question Captain Korzeniowski replied with unexpected frankness, "Self-confidence."

Ever since the love affair at Marseilles, if love affair there was, there had been no women in Conrad's life — except of course a series of landladies. He felt no desire for casual affairs and had had no prospect of supporting a wife until he reached the rank of captain. By now his fourteen pounds a week were jingling in his pocket, and an agreeable wife with a little money of her own might assuage his loneliness and ease the prospect of settling down into routine. Apparently Conrad was also carrying on a slight flirtation with a young girl called Alice Shaw, whom he described in one of his stories. He seems, however, to have been as much frightened as attracted by Alice, who was not yet seventeen. Mlle Eugénie, attractive if a trifle shallow, and experienced enough to give encouragement with tact, seemed a very possible wife for a man who only wanted a companion with whom he could relax between voyages. Captain Korzeniowski, however, was desperately shy of women. After all, since losing his mother at seven years old, he had lived exclusively in a male society, attracted by the opposite sex, but never able to establish intimate relations with a woman, unless briefly in Marseilles. Mlle Eugénie had coaxed him out of his shell a little way, but he could not bring himself to confess his hopes to her. He dreaded the moment when she must say "yes" or "no," and he could not face either. Ingeniously he hit on a solution which spared him this embarrassment. Immediately before leaving on the *Otago*, he called on Eugénie's brother with a formal offer for her hand, thus ensuring that if he was accepted, the courtship would proceed for a good while by letter.

Alas for his hopes! Mlle Eugénie had been engaged all along to a suitable business connection and would be married in a month or two. It seems incredible that Conrad had not even got far enough to find this out, but such was the case. His mortification was extreme, and he left on the *Otago* with the firm determination that he would not return to Mauritius to be laughed at. Whether this resolve was also due to the embarrassment of having preferred Eugénie's charms to those of Alice Shaw, we shall never know. After his marriage he did not mention Eugénie to his wife, but teased her about Alice.

6

Congo Fiasco

Conrad sailed for Melbourne in November 1888, where he picked up a cargo of wheat for Port Adelaide. Here he made a vain attempt to persuade the *Otago*'s owners to send her to the China seas instead of back to Mauritius. Failing, he threw up his command rather than face the Renoufs, putting forward the pretext that he must return to Europe because his Uncle Thaddeus had not long to live. Thaddeus had indeed written to say that he could not afford to take the cure abroad that his health needed, that he was making his will and leaving his nephew fifteen thousand roubles, and that he hoped Conrad could get Russian consent to his change of citizenship in time to pay him a final visit in Poland. Conrad, who could not have helped knowing that Thaddeus enjoyed making the worst of his health, did not rush off to Poland on his return to London in June 1889. On the contrary, he did his best to find another ship, and it was not until the following year that he visited his uncle. Meanwhile, his folly in resigning the captaincy of the *Otago* was underlined by fruitless efforts to obtain a command. One of his few friends in London was Adolf Krieger, the old Marseilles acquaintance who worked for Barr, Moering and Company and had originally interested Conrad in that firm. Krieger had shipping connections which enabled him to put Conrad in touch with an Antwerp firm trading with the West Indies; but months went by with no offer from them. Conrad, who was living a lonely life in lodgings, found time hanging heavy on his hands. He brooded a good deal, mulling over past experiences and finding his eighteen months on the *Vidar* productive of vivid reflections on Malay life and the clash of white and native cultures. The remoteness of the Berouw River concentrated these issues as though on a stage. The figure of Olmeijer, or Almayer, as the officers of the *Vidar* had called him, clad in short-sleeved cotton singlet and flapping pajama trousers printed with big yellow flowers on a blue ground, haunted Conrad's imagination. No doubt the re-creation of the little world on the Berouw offered a relief from the anxieties of the present.

In speaking of his own life, Conrad stresses the casualness with which he got up from the breakfast table one morning and rang the bell to have his dishes cleared away promptly. While the landlady's daughter fussed in and out, he stood smoking and gazing out of the window, not impatient, not yet entirely certain that he wanted to write a novel which seems to have been already entitled in his mind *Almayer's Folly*. He certainly had not planned the book in detail and had no idea of exchanging his sea career for that of author.

Yet, even though he pretends to have drifted into his vocation, he had cultivated literary interests since his childhood, not only through wide reading, but through the writing of elaborate letters, which had encouraged Thaddeus Bobrowski to suggest that he send articles from abroad to a Polish magazine. Recently, the captain of the *Vidar* had noticed how often he was writing. Furthermore, he told fascinating tales, based on experience but frequently adapted to suit the occasion. He was evidently creating constantly in his own mind, a process which led him to speak of his "pensive habits."

One important reason for Conrad's uncertain approach to *Almayer's Folly* lay in the fact that he did not sit down to write in his native language, nor yet in the French which he spoke fluently, but in English, which he had not learned till he was twenty and which he spoke with an accent to his dying day. It may seem strange that he made this choice, for we need not believe his later declaration that English was always his only possible language. Most probably, because his novel developed directly from experience, he found it as necessary to write it in English as to use the name of Almayer or describe the Berouw River with such fidelity that his old shipmates recognized people and landmarks. English had been the language used on the *Vidar;* and the "animated receptions of Malays, Arabs and half-castes" which he began to hold in his imagination every morning spoke to him in English or Malay. But however inevitable it was that he write of them in English, he was still using a language in which his speaking vocabulary had been limited by the society in which he had moved. Some years later when he was reading aloud from his second novel, he could hardly be understood because he mispronounced many words which he had picked up entirely from reading.

A beginning writer needs to discover his own mind and method of work. In Conrad's full-length novels, plot grew slowly, often changing the direction in which he was heading. It took him a long while to bring the characters of *Almayer's Folly* into relationships which flowed naturally from what he desired to say about them. Undecided whether he could or would finish, he had no thought of having embarked on a new profession. On the other hand, as months went by without a command and his restless nature led him to dream of other careers, *Almayer's Folly* did keep his attention steadily focused on the far places of the earth. Whether consciously or not, he could not help feeling that the Berouw River had provided experiences which were proving richer than all his adventures on the more traveled sea lanes of the world. In this way he grew ripe for a decision which was probably triggered by an incident which he records in his fiction. Walking down Fleet Street one day, "Charlie Marlow" stopped at a window displaying a map of central Africa, that very region which had been a big blank on Conrad's old school atlas, but which was now filled by, among other things, the Congo River, longest in Africa except the Nile and pouring out the greatest volume of water in the world except the Amazon. He remembered himself as a boy putting his finger on that empty map and saying, "When I grow up, I'm going *there*."

Why not? The Congo was a river as remote and rich in native life as the Berouw, but infinitely larger. Africa was much in the news, and the civilizing influence of the white man was talked of as the remedy for Africa's endemic slave trade, its starvation and disease, the horrible tyranny of its petty chieftains or witch doctors. That very clash of cultures which Conrad had observed on the Berouw was developing on a bigger scale on the Congo. Two characters, each greater in his own way than Tom Lingard, had started the process in Conrad's own lifetime — the explorer Henry Stanley, and Leopold II, King of Belgium.

In 1869, when Konrad Korzeniowski was eleven and reading avidly about exploration, an expedition commanded by Henry Morton Stanley was setting out to find the missionary and explorer David Livingstone, who had disappeared into darkest Africa in the hopes of discovering the ultimate source of the Nile. Whereas Livingstone wandered through Africa accompanied by a few native servants and essentially living off the land, Stanley's expedition, financed by the New York *Herald* as a newspaper stunt, set out with a long train of supplies carried by a small army of bearers. Thus when Stanley did find Livingstone in 1871, he had shown the effectiveness of a new kind of African exploration, financed on such a big scale that a return on their money was bound to be among the hopes of its backers.

Stanley's second expedition, an Anglo-American one supported by the *Daily Telegraph* of London as well as the *Herald,* was also designed to exploit public interest. Plunging into Africa from the east coast, the explorer vanished for three years, reappearing at the mouth of the Congo with tremendous news for the map-makers. Among other things, he had established the course of the Congo and disentangled its watershed from that of the Nile. He was greeted with deserved acclaim by the Western world and given a tremendous reception when he landed at Marseilles early in 1878, though Conrad, immersed at the time in his own personal crisis, failed to take part.

While Stanley was thus opening Africa to the interested gaze of Europeans, King Leopold of Belgium was considering how to turn the situation to his advantage. An able, but unscrupulous and unlovable man, Leopold had a passion, not precisely for himself, but for his dynasty. He had succeeded in 1865 to the throne of an inconsiderable little kingdom whose inhabitants thought more about trade than national glory. Unable to expand at the expense of his neighbors, Leopold dreamed of making his country, and particularly his capital, a model for Europe. In other words, he required vast sums for building schemes or cultural foundations, which he could not hope to finance out of Belgian taxes. This being the case, he looked around for an opportunity of making money and found it in Africa. It was clear to him that Belgium, whether she knew it or not, needed a colony.

Leopold started his activities in a kingly fashion by calling an international conference in Brussels to discuss methods of bringing the benefits of civilization to Africa. An association of distinguished persons was formed under his protection for this purpose. Accordingly, when Stanley landed at Marseilles in 1878 on his way to London, a royal emissary was waiting for him with an invitation to visit Brussels and lend a hand with the good work.

Stanley, whose health had been affected by the privations of his tremendous journey, refused the King's invitation for the moment. It was not to be supposed, however, that he could have passed through central Africa without perceiving the many miseries endured by Africans and wishing to better their lot. He was already appealing for missionaries and was eager to get British backing for an effort to open up the great river highway of the Congo. Such an enterprise would require capital, and Stanley was practical enough to know that trading profits would be necessary to it. However, his account of the riches of the Congo in ivory and rubber was not dazzling enough for British capitalists, who had plenty of colonies in which they could invest more securely. Accordingly, Stanley soon joined King Leopold in forming a company for development of the Congo, with a Belgian officer for president and most of its capital supplied by the King. As manager for this group, Stanley returned to the Congo to establish trading stations along the river with the intention of spreading civilization by these means. Flinging himself into his task with his customary energy, he cut a path through the jungle around the rapids which divide the upper Congo from the lower; and he actually had four small steamboats carried in sections along it to be launched on the upper river. Stanley would never have accomplished anything in Africa had he not been a driver as well as a leader of men. It is impossible to guess how many African lives were sacrificed to the cause of progress in these five years, and it is fair to say that the life expectancy of those who died was in any case exceedingly short. Nevertheless, a pattern was established on which Leopold's later agents were quick to improve.

Stanley worked for five years on the Congo; and Leopold

reaped the result of his efforts when, in 1885, he became king of the Congo Free State. This kingdom, which was his personal realm and quite independent of Belgium, lasted for twenty-three years, during which time it earned Leopold an enormous personal fortune, while reducing the population of the area by fifty percent. In 1890, when Conrad made up his mind to go to the Congo, there were already queer rumors about what was going on, though these were ignored by the Belgian press and, for diplomatic reasons, found small support elsewhere. Most people still thought of the enterprise as a civilizing one. Meanwhile, Stanley was once more in the news as leader of an expedition up the Congo and across primeval forest to rescue the Egyptian governor of Equatorial Africa, cut off from his base by an uprising. News of his meeting with Emin Pasha had arrived in January 1889, to be followed in April by detailed descriptions of fresh discoveries. His arrival on the east African coast in early December was greeted by telegrams from the Emperor of Germany, Queen Victoria, and the President of the United States. By February he was on his way to Europe and a series of receptions which almost put him on a par with royalty. No wonder a map of Africa was displayed in Fleet Street.

In a burst of enthusiasm, Conrad swept aside his unfinished novel and the disappointments of looking for a command. He had made up his mind to captain one of the river steamboats which Stanley had introduced to the upper Congo. Plans were being formed at the time for a Belgian expedition to clear up some geographical problems left unresolved by Stanley. The boats would certainly carry this group to Stanley Falls, the farthest limit of navigation and the point where trade stations ended. Adolf Krieger persuaded one of his Antwerp connections to write on his friend's behalf to Albert Thys, aide-de-camp to King Leopold and president of the corporation formed to develop the Congo. Meanwhile, Uncle Thaddeus, though skeptical about the whole venture, had reminded Conrad of a distant cousin, Alexander Poradowski, living in Brussels and married to a Frenchwoman who had written a couple of novels and had important social connections. After preliminary correspondence, Conrad arrived in Brussels only to find his cousin on his deathbed. Marguerite Poradowska, however, proved to be a warm and gracious woman, eleven years older than Conrad but still remarkable for beauty, who shared to the full his literary tastes. Starved of intelligent companionship, Conrad eagerly adopted her as an "aunt" and was soon writing her weekly letters.

Albert Thys held out hopes of a position for Conrad, but only after the lapse of some months. There was therefore no reason why he should not visit his uncle, since the Russians had finally recognized his change of nationality. It was twenty-three years since he had been to the Ukraine, yet all was just as he remembered. Even the coachman who drove the four-horse sleigh on his eight-hour journey from the nearest railroad station was the son of that Joseph who had let him take the reins and play with the big whip. Well he remembered how the sun set on the wintry plains, "dipping into the snow in full view as if it were setting on the sea." Darkness fell swiftly as he continued his journey until "out of the waste of a white earth joining a bestarred sky surged up black shapes, the clumps of trees about a village of the Ukrainian plain. A cottage or two glided by, a low interminable wall and then, glimmering and winking through a screen of fir trees, the lights of the master's house." The traveler had come home, and another servant who bore a family likeness to some remembered face unpacked his luggage, laying the manuscript of *Almayer's Folly* on a writing table which had been a present to his mother and her sister from that very Nicholas Bobrowski who had eaten Lithuanian dog during Napoleon's retreat from Moscow. But though Conrad had brought it along, he was not going to work on his novel.

"You won't have many hours to yourself while you are staying with me," remarked Uncle Thaddeus, hovering about him in the highest good humor. "I shall be always coming in for a chat."

Conrad spent a memorable two-month visit in Poland, hearing tales of his parents or enjoying meetings with half-forgotten cousins, some of whom now joined the list of his correspondents. Meanwhile, "Aunt Marguerite" threw herself enthusiastically into the task of getting her new nephew the job that he wanted. Either because she had influence, or because, as he says in "Heart of Darkness," a Congo captain had been speared in a quarrel over two black hens, an unexpected vacancy appeared. Passing through Belgium, Conrad found he had only time for forty-eight hours in London to collect equipment before visiting the offices of the company to sign his contract. He suggests that the atmosphere of this place gave him an uneasy feeling and writes of "Charlie Marlow" being asked by the doctor who gave him his physical examination, "Ever had any madness in your family?" But Marguerite Poradowska, on whom he called to offer his thanks, had no such misgivings. In Belgian circles the development of the Congo was productive of good for poor ignorant millions whom it was weaning from their "horrid ways." Naturally the company was run for a profit, but the laborer was worthy of his hire. No doubt the rhapsodies of Marguerite were unrealistic to a man already partway through a novel about the clash of white and native cultures. Nothing in Conrad's experiences, however, had prepared him for the realities of exploitation under the rule of Leopold.

He sailed in a French ship, the *Ville de Maceio* on May 10, 1890, with the unfinished *Almayer's Folly* still in his luggage. He was in the company of people returning to a dozen primitive ports on the west African coast, men without illusions, who lost no time in telling Conrad that sixty percent of the Belgian company's employees returned to Europe within six months, incapacitated by fever and dysentery. Sick people were sent home in a hurry so that they should not die in the Congo and spoil the health statistics, which were excellent. Conrad's chances of surviving the three-year stint for which he had been engaged did not sound great. He wrote to Marguerite Poradowska, wondering whether it might not be possible to transfer to the command of one of the company's ocean-going ships, plying between Boma, at the mouth of the Congo, and Antwerp. Nothing came of this suggestion; it was already too late. The *Ville de Maceio* plodded slowly down a coast which seemed to have no features except a dark green line of jungle fringed with white surf which was occasionally interrupted by tiny settlements, where they landed customhouse clerks to work in some tin shed beneath a flagpole, or soldiers, presumably to guard them.

"Once, I remember, we came upon a man-of-war anchored off the coast," says Charlie Marlow, no doubt describing this adventure very much as Conrad experienced it. "There wasn't even a shed there, and she was shelling the bush. It appears the French had one of their wars going on thereabouts. Her ensign dropped limp like a rag; the muzzles of the long six-inch guns stuck out all over the low hull; the greasy, slimy swell swung her up lazily and let her down, swaying her thin masts. In the empty immensity of earth, sky, and water, there she was, incomprehensible, firing into a continent."

At Boma, Conrad disembarked into a smaller boat for Matadi, which was about forty miles higher upstream, and the furthest navigable point of the lower Congo. Matadi was quite a large place with 170 Europeans in it, noisy with the sound of the rapids above and busy with the beginnings of a railroad which was intended to run across to the upper Congo. Since at this point the Congo forms a wide lake surrounded by hills, Matadi was necessarily built on a steep slope. Ascending this, Charlie Marlow describes as first impressions things which may have taken Conrad some time to assimilate. There was a boiler abandoned in the grass, a railway truck with its wheels in the air, a stack of rusty rails, an occasional detonation as the cliff was blasted to make a place for the railroad. He had his first sight of a chain gang. "Six black men advanced in a file, toiling up the path. They walked erect and slow, balancing small baskets full of earth on their heads, and the clink kept time with their footsteps. Black rags were wound about their loins, and the short ends behind waggled to and fro like tails. I could see every rib, the joints of their limbs were like knots in a rope; each had an iron collar on his neck, and all were connected together with a chain whose bights swung between them, rhythmically clinking."

Not caring for this sight, Marlow struck off the path with the intention of making for the shade of a grove of trees. Beneath it he found in abandoned attitudes the broken-down laborers who had withdrawn to die. "They were dying slowly — it was very clear. They were . . . nothing but black shadows of disease and starvation, lying confusedly in a greenish gloom. Brought from all the recesses of the coast in all the legality of time contracts, lost in uncongenial surroundings, fed on unfamiliar food, they sickened, became inefficient, and were then allowed to crawl away and rest."

Such were the signs of Leopold's rule in Matadi. The white men were dominated by the most ruthless among them, whose only object was to make their profit before the climate killed them. The rest were a varied group of misfits, people who had got out of Europe just ahead of trouble, a few idealists lost in their surroundings, idlers sent out to make good by their relations, or rugged adventurers impatient of civilized routines. Conrad, who began at this point to keep a diary, noted in it that he intended to avoid acquaintances and that social life in Matadi largely consisted in speaking ill of others. He met, in fact, only one congenial person, an Irish adventurer who, as British consul at Boma thirteen years later, was to make a devastating report to his government which eventually led to a change in the administration of the Congo.

Conrad spent a couple of unhappy weeks in Matadi before setting out with a certain M. Harou and thirty-one bearers on the two-hundred-mile trek to Kinshassa, which was the steamship base on the upper Congo. The countryside through which they passed was fairly open, but rough and hilly, intersected by ravines which carried streams into the Congo. Days were unpleasantly hot; nights were cold and thick with mosquitoes. They would start about dawn, protected by the morning mists from the sun, and pass through country which was generally deserted, though occasionally they came to a native market where they bought eggs or chickens. About noon, when it became too hot for travel, they stopped at some dirty camping place which was only too often insufficiently supplied with muddy water. They rested at one clean and comfortable Protestant mission and met one white traveler, an official inspecting, or so he said, the condition of the road. The only evidence of his activities was the dead body of a native, presumably shot. Harou, unhealthily fat, was ill from the start and had a habit of fainting on hot hillsides miles away from shade or water. He had to be carried a great deal of the way in a hammock, which was the cause of rows with the bearers, who complained with some justice that he was far too heavy. Conrad himself seems to have been remarkably resistant to malaria and tropical diseases during a journey which lasted thirty-six days. He complained of feeling seedy or of nights without sleep because of the mosquitoes. He arrived, however, on his own feet and physically able to take command of the steamer waiting for him.

Alas for his hopes! The *Florida* had been badly damaged and was undergoing repairs which, considering the remoteness of Kinshassa and the general inefficiency of everything being done by the company, might be expected to last an indefinite time. For the present, he was attached as a supernumerary to the *Roi des Belges*, which was going upriver to collect the company's agent at Stanley Falls, who was seriously ill. Since this arrangement would give Conrad a chance to learn the navigation of the river before taking over his command, it made some sense. By now, however, logic made small impression on his exasperated nerves. He wrote off a letter of complaint to Thaddeus, who replied in effect, "You *would* do it!" adding that to get himself worked up was bad for his liver, while to break his three-year contract so soon would be bad for his record. Before this irritating answer arrived, Conrad had left in the *Roi des Belges*, accompanied by Camille Delcommune, who had just been made acting director of the company in the Congo.

In essence, the expedition went fairly well. The captain became ill, so that Conrad had a chance to take over command. They duly rescued Georges Klein, the company's agent, who died, however, on the way back. Conrad smoked his pipe below Stanley Falls, pretty much on the spot where his childish finger had rested on the atlas years ago. Between himself and Delcommune, however, a real antipathy had arisen. Conrad despised the man, perhaps no more than he did all the company's agents; but his manner did not endear

him to his superior. As he admitted to Marguerite Poradowska, his rising disgust at the unashamed display of human
baseness which he daily witnessed was too much for his
nerves. He could not bring himself to be agreeable.

The result of his attitude was very soon felt. The Belgian
expedition which had been preparing to explore one of the
tributaries of the Congo was to be commanded by Alexandre
Delcommune, Camille's elder brother, who naturally received a bad report about Conrad. Thus, though he had
been supposed to command the steamer which would take
them on their journey of some ten months, it soon became
obvious that he had not the slightest prospect of doing so and
escaping out of the sordid atmosphere of the company's operations into a genuine share in exploration. Camille Delcommune bluntly informed him that there was no reason
why the company's agents on the spot should grant him
anything that was not explicitly spelled out in his contract.
The *Florida* would not be ready for nine months at least;
and it was obvious that if Delcommune could find a way of
preventing Conrad from commanding her then, he was
eager to do so. Once more Conrad asked Marguerite Poradowska to use her influence and get him transferred to one
of the ships which plied between Belgium and Boma, where,
if still a slave to his three-year contract with the infamous
company, he would at least be out of sight and hearing.

Marguerite prepared to do her best, but by the time she
got his letter, Conrad was far too ill to care about the result.
Malaria and dysentery, the killing diseases of the Congo,
soon made it imperative to hurry him home for the sake of
the health statistics. Luckily, though it was not possible to

travel upstream from Matadi to Kinshassa, one could get back down the rapids in native canoes. The journey was not without risk, but Conrad was far too sick to care how it ended or whether *Almayer's Folly*, which still made a part of his diminishing baggage, survived the trip. He arrived intact at Boma in plenty of time for the steamer which was going to take him home, but hardly appreciated his good luck. On the contrary, the wait gave him plenty of time to wish himself dead.

THIRD LIFE

The English Novelist

7

First Novel

CONRAD got back to England in January 1891, after four months in the Congo which had permanently ruined his health and affected his spirits. Malaria soon led to gout, a recurrent and extremely painful rheumatic disease, some of whose causes still remain obscure. An accompaniment of gout is nervous irritation, which in turn affects the recurrence of its symptoms. Thus to his uncle, confusing the serious with the trivial, he complained that one of his legs was greatly swollen and that he was going bald. To Marguerite, he wrote from hospital that his left leg, right arm and general digestion were affected. A couple of months later he told her that his nerves were completely on edge. He was passing through a nervous and physical breakdown brought on both by disease and by the shock of exposure to the worst side of human nature in the Congo. In May he went to take a cure at a hydropathic resort in Switzerland, where he recovered sufficiently to take up work again on *Almayer's Folly*. This did not, however, mark the beginning of a permanent recovery. His impression of evil as a part of human nature which is only smoothed over by ideals, laws, or conventions remained with him for life, intensifying the dark moods to which he previously had been subject. Meanwhile gout, waiting to spring on him at every major crisis, was soon to unfit him for pursuit of the profession which he had worked so hard to master.

His money was running low as he returned to England to look for a job. As usual when desperate, he suggested one business scheme after another to Uncle Thaddeus, provoking that cautious man to write him another letter about the ups and downs of the Korzeniowski temperament. Thaddeus was also alarmed enough to point out that Marguerite Poradowska was eleven years older than her "nephew," and that a flirtation between them could come to no good. Actually, Conrad's letters to Marguerite at this time were about as formal in tone as those to his uncle. Conrad, who had so few companions he could talk to, was using both of them as an emotional outlet.

Gradually he began to feel better; and in November he was offered the position of first mate on the *Torrens*, one of the best of the Australian wool clippers. He hesitated on account of his health, but was urged by the captain, Walker Cope, to take the job. For Conrad, this was a step down in rank; but the *Torrens* was a famous ship which would have looked well on anybody's record. Allowing himself to be persuaded, Conrad sailed for Port Adelaide at the end of November, returning in the middle of 1892. The activity

had suited his emotional needs, and his health had proved
adequate to the job. His dependence on Marguerite Poradowska was evidently less, and he was able to write to his
uncle fairly cheerfully.

The *Torrens* always carried passengers, who were attracted
by her outstanding reputation. As Conrad left on his second
trip, she had aboard a young man called Jacques who, after
taking first-class honors at Cambridge, had contracted tuberculosis and had been ordered to take a long sea voyage.
Conrad, always starved for intelligent company, got on well

Conrad (center, top) as first mate of the *Torrens,* with
his second and third mates and three cabin boys

enough with Jacques to ask his opinion of *Almayer's Folly*, whose existence was his most closely guarded secret. Jacques took the manuscript away to read it and returned it to the author without a word.

"Well, what do you say?" demanded Conrad anxiously. "Is it worth finishing?"

"Distinctly." Jacques coughed a little.

"Were you interested?"

"Very much."

"Now let me ask you one more thing: Is the story quite clear to you as it stands?"

Jacques looked him in the face with a surprised expression. "Perfectly."

With rare understanding, Jacques dropped the subject; and Conrad, too sensitive for criticism, however intelligent, did not pursue it. He had the encouragement which was what he wanted.

Curiously enough, Jacques was joined on the return voyage by two other passengers who might have seemed fit for Conrad's confidence. They were a pair of young Oxford graduates who had taken a year off to visit the South Seas and were returning by way of Australia and Cape Town. Ted Sanderson, the son of the headmaster of a well-known school for younger boys, was to have a varied career in South Africa and England. John Galsworthy, son of a wealthy lawyer, was to become Conrad's chief literary rival.

A novelist very much in the English tradition of the authors of *Tom Jones* and *Vanity Fair*, Galsworthy is so different from Conrad that admirers of the one nearly always belittle the other. Nor did either quite understand the other's excellence, however intelligently he tried to praise it. Well-to-do from birth, Galsworthy could afford to devote himself to writing without any thought of what he might earn. Success came to him earlier than to Conrad, though he was the younger by ten years. Their manners of living were to prove as different as their temperaments. Galsworthy was a town dweller from choice, whereas Conrad usually buried himself in the country, too ill or too hard up to visit London. Both became devoted husbands, but to wives who had nothing in common. In fact, when the mate of the *Torrens* struck up an acquaintance with a rather conventional young man who vaguely wished he had the gift of writing, there was no reason to suppose that their friendship would endure. Galsworthy's comment at the time is admiring, but casual: "The first mate is a Pole called Conrad and is a capital chap, though queer to look at; he is a man of travel and experience in many parts of the world and has a fund of yarns on which I draw freely." As it happened, however, Galsworthy had the quality of faithfulness, while Conrad was hungry for friendship. Thus, strangely enough, two men whose future careers were bound to bring them many friends in common, were intimate before those careers had even started.

After Conrad's death many years later, Galsworthy wrote a description of the mate of the *Torrens* which gives a vivid picture of Conrad near the end of his sea career. He first met him in Port Adelaide, he says, superintending the stowage of the cargo. "Very dark he looked in the burning sunlight, tanned, with a peaked brown beard, almost black hair, and dark brown eyes over which the lids were deeply folded. He was thin, not tall, his arms very long, his shoulders broad, his

head set rather forward. He spoke to me with a strong foreign accent. He seemed to me strange on an English ship.
For fifty-six days I sailed in his company.

"The chief mate bears the real burden of a sailing ship.
All the first night he was fighting a fire in the hold. None
of us seventeen passengers knew of it till long after. It was
he who had most truck with the tail of that hurricane off
the Leeuwin, and later with another storm: a good seaman,
watchful of the weather, quick in handling the ship, considerate with the apprentices. We had an unhappy Belgian
youth among them, who took unhandily to the sea and
dreaded going aloft. Conrad compassionately spared him all

John
Galsworthy

he could. With the crew he was popular; they were individuals to him, not a mere gang; and he would (later) talk of this or that among them, especially of old Andy, the sailmaker; 'I liked that fellow, you know.'

"With the young second mate, a cheerful, capable young seaman, very English, he was friendly; and respectful, if faintly ironic with his whiskered, stout old captain. Evening watches in fine weather we spent on the poop. Ever the great teller of a tale, he had already nearly twenty years of tales to tell . . .

"On that ship he told of life, not literature. On my last evening he asked me . . . to his cabin, and I remember feeling that he outweighed for me all the other experience of that voyage. Fascination was Conrad's great characteristic — the fascination of vivid expressiveness and zest, of his deeply affectionate heart, and his far-ranging, subtle mind. He was extraordinarily perceptive and receptive."

By the time Conrad got back to London, difficulties were closing in on him again. Captain Cope, who had failed to make the record passages of his predecessor, talked in disgust of throwing up his job and going into steam. Conrad had hopes of the captaincy, should his health not prove too uncertain. Meanwhile, Uncle Thaddeus, once more gloomy about his own health, suggested that Conrad pay him another final visit. He did so, only to become more ill than the patient and to retire to bed. Returning to London, he found that Captain Cope was staying with the *Torrens* and, either out of disappointment or because he doubted whether he was physically fit, resigned his job. In December he learned that the steamship *Adowa*, chartered to carry French emigrants to Canada, needed a second officer who spoke French. It was another step down, but life on a steamer was less strenuous. He proceeded to Rouen, where the *Adowa* was tied up, only to find that the Franco-Canadian company involved was in financial trouble. No emigrants arrived.

"What are you always scribbling there, if it's fair to ask?" inquired the third officer, who solaced his own idle hours on the *Adowa* by playing the banjo. Conrad did not answer him, but turned the manuscript of *Almayer's Folly* face down.

The steamship company failed; and after some weeks in Rouen, Conrad went back to London, where he shortly received the news that his uncle was dead. It was a real blow, severing the one strong link with his childhood. Uncle Thaddeus may have preached a little too often, but for years he had been the only person who really loved Conrad and in a certain sense understood him. Even after ten years in England, he had no one to console him but Marguerite Poradowska, to whom he confided that he felt as though he himself had died with his uncle.

Joblessness and the uncertainty of his health added to Conrad's depression, but he was writing again and dashed off a triumphant letter to Marguerite in April 1893: "I regret to announce the death of Mr. Kaspar Almayer, which took place this morning at 3 A.M.

"It's finished."

It was, yet it was not. Ted Sanderson and his mother were working over Conrad's English, which lapsed occasionally into French idiom or simple error. He himself was revising the story with alterations and additions. By July it was actually ready to be sent to the publisher Fisher Unwin. Long experience with the name Korzeniowski had led its owner to suggest people call him Conrad, from which the name of Joseph Conrad naturally followed. Since, however, he never used the "Joseph" except when he needed two names for a signature, he soon became "Conrad" to everyone alike. His new English friends, the Sandersons and the Galsworthys, all called him Conrad and introduced him to their acquaintances by this name. Thus in a certain sense it did for him as Christian name and surname, soon superseding Korzeniowski entirely, except of course in his sea profession, where his true legal name was on his papers.

The manuscript which he sent to Fisher Unwin was handed over to a young man called Edward Garnett to read. Garnett, a perceptive literary critic, soon became the discoverer and promoter of most of the best young writers of his day. He was only twenty-six when he detected the unusual qualities of *Almayer's Folly*, which in spite of its tropical setting is by no means the conventional rover's yarn, but rather the study of a failure told unsentimentally, almost objectively, and yet with a deep appreciation that Almayer for all his faults is a man whose capacity for suffering is as great as that of another. Only rarely do we feel real sympathy for him; but in perceiving him as a man not strong enough for his circumstances, we are led to compare him with the struggling trees of the jungle smothered by creepers, with the rotting piles of his wharf, with the flotsam rolled down by the river. Thus we pity him and free him from blame, even while we cannot like him. Later critics have pointed out that Conrad's writing was too wordy and contained too many purple passages having little to do with the action of the story. They have said that his understanding of Malays was superficial and that this affects his attitude toward the meeting of two cultures. They have blamed his love scenes for being stilted and picked out other faults of inexperience. Garnett, however, perceived that *Almayer* was a remarkable first novel, displaying an originality which seemed all the greater because the literary masters who had shaped Conrad's style were French rather than English.

On Garnett's recommendation, Fisher Unwin bought the copyright of *Almayer's Folly* outright for twenty pounds. Garnett, who did not in the course of his work as a publisher's reader have any contact with the authors whose books he recommended, expressed a special interest in meeting this unusual sea captain. Unwin therefore arranged a meeting at his club, in whose formal atmosphere he led the conversation onto political or literary figures who were all unknown to Conrad. Polite and deferential, as was his habit with strangers, Conrad grew more and more abrupt in his answers, unceasingly shifting his feet one over the other until Garnett became quite mesmerized by the sight. Finally, when Unwin politely referred to his next book, he could bear it no longer. "I don't expect to write again," he retorted clearly and coldly. "It is likely that I shall soon be going to sea."

Luckily, at this juncture Unwin got up to greet some friends, leaving Garnett to protest earnestly, "You have written one book. It is very good. Why not write another?"

In the privacy of his own lodgings, Conrad was already at work on another, though it was not at the moment going well. No doubt Unwin had frightened him into a resolution to stop writing at once, which it is possible he might have done temporarily. Garnett succeeded in making him feel that at any rate *one* other book might not be beyond his powers. Conrad was soon settled in his own mind as a professional author.

8

Putting Down Roots

Conrad could hardly support himself long on the twenty pounds he received from Fisher Unwin and told his friends that he was too old to start authorship by starving in a garret. His efforts, however, to find another ship were unavailing. Undoubtedly, the higher he got in his profession, the more his foreign manner and appearance were against him. Sailing ships were rapidly giving way to steam, on which he had little experience. No one wanted an officer liable to be laid up with a painful attack of gout at any moment. Finally it is possible that his record was unsatisfactory to shipowners who were looking for a man who would stay with them for more than one or two voyages. Unemployed, Conrad worked steadily on *An Outcast of the Islands*, despite recurrent bouts of illness or depression, and had nearly finished it by the time *Almayer's Folly* was published in April 1895.

On the whole, *Almayer's Folly* was received well by the

reviewers. Only one or two said "genius," but all said "promise" and hoped there would be more from the same pen.
This enthusiasm was not shared by the general public, suspicious of the exotic setting and preferring the familiar to the
experimental. Since Conrad was receiving no royalties from
the book, he was more apt to be encouraged by reviews than
depressed by the absence of sales. He put the last touches on
An Outcast of the Islands, eking out his resources by a couple
of successful strokes of business.

One of his oldest friends in London was Fountain Hope,
who had been introduced by Krieger and was an amateur
yachtsman who kept a sailboat on the Thames estuary. Naturally Conrad, with plenty of time on his hands at this period, went cruising with him. Hope's brother-in-law had a
claim to ownership of a South African gold mine, but was in
danger of being swindled out of it by a French company.
The situation called for someone fluent in French and with
connections in Paris, where Marguerite Poradowska was
currently living. Conrad undertook the negotiation, was
successful, and was compensated by two hundred shares.
This in turn led to a chance to sell more South African gold-
mining shares on commission. Unfortunately, he also invested in them the legacy Uncle Thaddeus had left him.

By September he was able to finish *An Outcast of the
Islands*, which he had sold to Fisher Unwin for fifty pounds
down and 12½ percent royalty on sales. Triumphantly he
wrote to Garnett:

"It is my painful duty to inform you of the sad death of
Mr. Peter Willems, late of Rotterdam and Macassar, who has
been murdered on the 16th inst at 4 p.m. while the sun shone

joyously and the barrel organ sang on the pavement."

The subject of *An Outcast of the Islands* is the destruction of a white man by his passion for a Malay woman. The self-respect of Peter Willems had already been undermined by a dishonest act, so that he was soon induced to betray his friends and benefactor for the sake of Aissa. The action is set on the Berouw River a few years earlier than *Almayer*, though Almayer is also a character in the story. Longer than the earlier novel and in some ways more ambitious, *An Outcast of the Islands* has the same defects and virtues. Actually, Conrad had learned a good deal, but the identical setting and characters tended to force him into similar methods of dealing with them, making the likeness between the two books most apparent. Published in 1896, it was received favorably, though the enthusiasm of novelty was naturally lacking. However, a distinguished new critic joined the chorus, calling *An Outcast* "perhaps the finest piece of fiction that has been published this year." After such a start, it did not matter that he went on to criticize the style as horribly wordy. Conrad wrote to thank him for his appreciation and to his immense joy discovered that the writer was H. G. Wells, then at the height of his reputation as an author of science fiction. Conrad was beginning to make important friends.

Meanwhile, he had abandoned the Berouw River in favor of a new novel to be called *The Sisters*, based on some of his Marseilles experiences but set in Paris. It started badly, and after a while he laid it aside. He was still busy trying to get to sea, and he was courting — an additional reason for needing a source of steady income.

The girl whom he was making up his mind to marry was so ordinary that she seemed a strange choice for Conrad. Jessie George was a twenty-three-year-old typist who had been introduced to him by Hope, a friend of her family. Her father, who had died about three years before, had been a bookseller; he had left a wife and ten children, Jessie being one of the eldest. Luckily her earnings were not essential to the family, but she could bring no money to her marriage. In person, Jessie was a plump girl not more than passably good-looking whose outstanding characteristic was an unshakable evenness of temper. In tastes she was entirely domestic, an excellent cook, devoted to small children, but without any intellectual pretensions whatsoever.

Many find it difficult to understand what Conrad saw in Jessie, but certain guesses can be made about it. He was increasingly lonely, especially as the long months went by without a chance of getting away to sea. It is possible that after his uncle's death he did propose to Marguerite Poradowska; but if so, she had refused him. Nor is it certain that so sensitive and irritable a man would have been happy with an intelligent critic installed under his own roof. Jessie's placid determination to make him comfortable in the most unpromising surroundings soothed his nerves.

According to her account, Jessie first met Conrad between his two voyages on the *Torrens*. He was fifteen years older than she, and his exaggerated foreign courtesies rather took her breath away. They were followed by a box of flowers and a card signed Konrad Korzeniowski, which she had some difficulty in connecting with the "Captain Conrad" to whom she had been introduced. Many months later, as she was sitting in the family living room sewing and idly watching the funeral processions go by to the great cemetery at the end of the road, she saw a cab drive up, scanning the numbers for the right address. Before it had so much as stopped, an immaculate figure swung open the door and jumped impetuously out. Captain Conrad, back from Australia, had come to invite Jessie and her mother to dine with him in a restaurant where he had already in full confidence ordered dinner.

Blinded by the difference between their ages, Mrs. George, who did not like foreigners, never wondered why Jessie began going out with the Polish captain, usually taking thirteen-year-old Ethel as chaperone. When *Almayer* came out, Jessie received a copy, and about this time she was drafted into reading aloud from the manuscript of *An Outcast*. There was nothing loverlike about Conrad's manner on the occasion: "Disregard those corrections . . . that passage is not going to stand . . . Never mind . . . start three lines lower down — now overleaf, overleaf.

"Oh, do speak distinctly. If you're tired, say so. Don't eat your words. You English are all alike; you make the same sound for every letter."

Mrs. George might have been reassured; but several months later the acquaintance had progressed sufficiently for Jessie to meet Conrad alone at Victoria Station, where he appeared in a highly nervous state, venting his feelings by finding fault with her hat, her dress, and her general lack of color. Beckoning a cab, he took her to the National Gallery, where he steered her to a seat without looking at the pictures and said abruptly, "Look here, my dear, we had better get

married and out of this. Look at the weather. We will get
married at once and get over to France. How soon can you
be ready? In a week — a fortnight?"

Jessie was not taken by surprise, but she was indeed rather
startled when her lover urged that there was need for hurry
because he did not expect to live long. Her shock was nothing to that felt by her mother, whose comment on Conrad
was "Oh dear, one could never take him for an Englishman,
and he doesn't look French either." Mrs. George came tot-
tering home from a dinner at which the news had been
broken to her and announced to her family: "Jessie has engaged herself to Captain Conrad, the foreign sailor — and . . .
will be married in six weeks' time. Let me get to bed . . ."
Her eldest daughter led her upstairs, no doubt repeating to
herself some of her incoherent protests to Jessie. "He wants
no family! Then why marry? What illness does he expect
to die of?" Jessie, who had a sense of humor which, strangely
enough for so placid a person, was rather malicious, fills her
reminiscences with similar stories.

The marriage took place before a registrar in March 1896,
with Krieger, Hope, and Mrs. George as witnesses. It was
followed by a lunch and a cake-cutting ceremony at Jessie's
home, at which all the family dissolved into tears, causing
Conrad to exclaim: "Good heavens, if I had known this
would happen, I — well, I would never have married you."

The happy couple retired to Conrad's lodgings, where
Jessie complained she spent most of the night packing her
husband's clothes and helping him answer letters of congratulation, which he insisted they both go out to mail at
two in the morning. Next day, Mrs. George came around

for lunch and saw them off on the boat train for France. Jessie, who had been strictly ordered by her husband not to weep, well knew that her mother's feelings would be hurt if she shed no tears at parting. Waiting, therefore, until the train had begun to pull out, she turned away from Conrad to wave goodbye, while holding a handkerchief unobstrusively to dry eyes. The marriage had begun.

The Conrads started life together in a rented cottage on the Ile Grande off the coast of Brittany, a remote and primitive place which had the merit of being inexpensive. A few weeks before the wedding, Conrad, who had invested most of his little inheritance in the South African gold mines, received news that it was lost. He had already started a new novel, "The Rescuer" (later published as *The Rescue*), in which he had introduced as his hero the Rajah Laut under the name of Tom Lingard. The responsibility, however, of supporting a wife out of a profession which paid him little had induced him to try a popular style which did not suit him. While he wrestled with this, Jessie, whose marriage had demonstrated a love of adventure which no one would have guessed from her placid demeanor, was busying herself rescuing her husband's manuscripts, typing what he wrote on what surely must have been the most primitive machine ever used for this purpose, and making their cold and drafty quarters as comfortable as could be done without expending any money. She evidently faced the circumstances of her marriage to a very odd man with a determination which was only shaken when he came down with an attack of malaria complicated by gout. Jessie, who had hardly heard of gout and had not taken her husband's talk of dying seriously, was terrified by his raving for three days in Polish, and then turning on her in English later, reducing her to tears.

Stuck in *The Rescue*, Conrad turned to short stories, producing "The Idiots," a tale suggested by an idiot family in Brittany, "The Lagoon," another Malay story, and "An Outpost of Progress," based on experiences in the Congo. None of these shows Conrad at his best, but by September he had started on his first major work, *The Nigger of the Narcissus*.

After about six months, the Conrads decided to return to England, finding a stone cottage off the coast of Brittany too cold for winter, especially for a man with rheumatic troubles. They settled in a cottage in Essex, near the Hopes and convenient for sailing. Conrad sent Jessie ahead to buy furniture, giving her fifty pounds, which proved not nearly enough. Jessie's mother, drafted to help, could not conceal her annoyance when her impractical son-in-law decided to make a celebration of the occasion of their settling into their first real house. He wrote to announce the day that he was coming, telling Jessie to have the dinner all ready, to have the maid in the kitchen, and to receive him in her drawing room instead of rushing out to greet him in the hall. He even sent her five pounds for a pretty negligee, which Jessie promptly spent for bedding. He duly came, accompanied by a delivery boy bearing fruit and flowers, but Jessie was unable to play her part; while looking around him, he took a violent dislike to the cheap furnishings and to the house itself, describing it, evidently not without reason, as a "damned jerry-built hutch." It was damp and cold, and the chimney smoked. In any case he was determined not to be happy in it. Presently Jessie discovered an Elizabethan farmhouse without plumbing, electricity, gas, or any modern convenience, but at least built to last and surrounded by open land. They moved the following March, by which time Conrad had completed *The Nigger of the Narcissus*.

The Nigger of the Narcissus, with its brilliant character sketches and its tremendous storm at sea, makes fine reading matter, but Conrad has much more than a straight story to tell. The ship is a human community whose strength is tested not merely by the storms which sailors must meet, but by the characters which go to make up a crew. The dying black man faces a moment which all fear, because survival is the ultimate reason why any crew hangs together. On the *Narcissus*, however, death and malingering have become confused, in part by the actions of the Negro, and in part by the presence of another man, who has no sense of duty to the group. The community is broken up more easily by its own weaknesses than by the storm. The universality of this theme is actually strengthened by its deliberate limitation. By setting the voyage of the *Narcissus* in a framework which emphasizes the chance gathering of this particular group and its breakup after the voyage, Conrad isolates a single human experience just as if he had directed his flashlight on it in the dark. For this reason, while we do apply its lessons to larger communities, we recognize that so small an incident cannot supply every answer. *The Nigger of the Narcissus* becomes a satisfying whole, achieving what it set out to do, no more, no less.

Fisher Unwin had offered no better terms for a short-story volume than he had for *An Outcast of the Islands*. When

Conrad rejected this as insufficient, Garnett, as Unwin's employee, was in an awkward position to help. This did not, however, prevent him from introducing Conrad to the London editor of Heinemann's, who was shown the first part of *The Nigger* and liked it so well that he persuaded the *New Review* to serialize it before publication. *The Rescue* was still stuck, but Conrad was working on another book of shorter stories. Magazines were beginning to take an interest in his work: *Blackwood's* accepted "Karain," while *Cosmopolis* agreed to publish "An Outpost of Progress."

By the middle of 1897, although the Conrads' marriage had settled down well, considering the differences of temperament involved, Jessie had begun to perceive how much Conrad suffered by isolation from men who shared his intellectual gifts. No doubt this had always been so, but the routine of a ship had given occupation or made demands which did not depend on intellectual stimulus. The Conrads had settled in Essex to be near the Hopes, who were not always there. Conrad did not like walking, for which indeed his gout had probably unfitted him. In fact, he had no taste for any country occupation except his Sunday yachting parties with Hope, when gout did not interfere. Thus, though he desperately needed relaxation from the tension with which he worked, he seldom found any. Galsworthy, Garnett, or Sanderson would come down for occasional weekends from London, at which Conrad would cheer up, demand special menus which he thought his friends would like, and fill his day with little expeditions to the general store for some delicacy which had been forgotten. When they came, he was almost too glad to see them and indulged in a positive orgy of good conversation lasting well into the night. After his visitors left, he would progress well with his writing, only to lapse after a few days into despair.

Many of his worries were still financial. Conrad had no personal extravagances except cigarettes; but he was prodigal when entertaining, and friends were necessary to his temperament. About this time, another piece of extravagance came his way which forced him to borrow twenty pounds from his Polish friends in Cardiff. Jessie was not well and soon discovered that she was going to have a child. Since Conrad was already at his wits' end financially, his announcement of this prospect to his friends was by no means triumphant; while Jessie, too, had doubts. She had made up her mind to make a success of marriage with a man who was hungry for affection and tender care. Feeling herself mother as well as wife to her husband, she was uncertain what the effect would be when she divided attention and duties.

Meanwhile, Conrad's books were slowly bringing contacts with interesting men. Among these was Stephen Crane, the young American author of *The Red Badge of Courage*, which he had published two years before at the age of twenty-four. Conrad and Crane had the same United States publisher, while the *Red Badge* and the *Nigger* both took as their theme the reaction of individuals in a group assembled for a specific purpose. It was inevitable that the two books should be compared and that the authors should meet when Crane arrived in England. Introduced at a luncheon by Pawling, Heinemann's London agent, they talked till four o'clock and then, as Pawling had an appointment, wandered

out into the streets of London still talking, had dinner together, and continued conversation till late in the evening.

Primarily Crane was a reporter, earning enormous sums,
which he spent even faster than he received them, aided and
abetted by his mistress, Cora Stewart, who was unable to get
a divorce to marry him. Crane and Cora were endlessly
hospitable on a grand scale, and the Conrads were soon
numbered among their visitors. In fact, a journey to the
Cranes' in February 1898 was the first piece of travel ever
undertaken by Borys Alfred Conrad, who had been born a
month before. With her usual delight in telling tales against
her husband, Jessie says that Conrad, who had bought the
party first-class tickets, was only prepared to travel in company with herself and sister Dora if they undertook to
behave as though he were a stranger who had nothing in the
world to do with that baby. After a time, Borys started to
cry, causing the other passengers, all of them ladies, to apologize to him for the noise, taking him for an unattached male.
At this point Dora let the cat out of the bag by asking him
to get down the case with the baby's bottle from the rack
above his head. Everybody suppressed smiles; and Conrad,
enduring their amusement stony-faced, told Garnett when
he arrived, "I hate babies."

He was still struggling with *The Rescue*, now sold to
McClure's Magazine, which weighed on his conscience. "I've
obtained a ton of cash from a Yank under what strikes me
as false pretences," he wrote. "He *thinks* that the book he
bought will be finished in July, while I know it is a physical
and intellectual impossibility to even approach the end by
that date. He sends in regular checks which is — according

to his lights — right: but I pocket them serenely, which — according to my lights — looks uncommonly like a swindle on my part." Driven by a sense of obligation, he sat at his writing desk eight hours a day, producing "three sentences, which I erase before I leave the table in despair." Once more he abandoned the novel in favor of a more congenial idea, in the course of which he invented perhaps his most famous character, Charlie Marlow.

Marlow is a kind of English Conrad, a wanderer on the face of the earth who has a fund of stories to tell. The first of these, written at this time, was "Youth," which was told by Marlow in a mood of nostalgia in an after-dinner session. The trick, for it is no more, enables Conrad to heighten the romance of the story by contrast with the older man that Marlow has become. "Oh, the glamour of youth! Oh, the fire of it, more dazzling than the flames of the burning ship, throwing a magic light on the wide earth, leaping audaciously to the sky, presently to be quenched by time, more cruel, more pitiless, more bitter than the sea — and like the flames of the ship surrounded by an impenetrable night." Speaking as Marlow, Conrad could let himself go, expressing his own mixed emotions through the narrator, whose comments are as much a part of the tale as the events themselves. "Youth" did not take long to write because on Marlow's lips it must have been little altered from one of those stories told on the poop of the *Torrens* which had made John Galsworthy a friend for life.

Conrad's financial position was looking worse than ever, and he made a last desperate effort to get to sea. A Scottish friend gave introductions, while he himself went up to Glasgow to make a round of shipowners there. The Glasgow literary society entertained him; but shipowners did not know what to make of a novel-writing captain except that his devotion to their interests would only endure as long as he needed their money. He returned, poorer by the expense of the trip, to face the hopeless problem of *The Rescue*.

In the fall of 1898, the Conrads went to stay with Garnett in Surrey and were introduced to a young man of twenty-four who had published a few fairytales and a first novel. Ford Madox Hueffer's father, a German music critic, had married the daughter of a well-known Victorian artist, Ford Madox Brown. Since another daughter had married William Rossetti, brother of the artist and poet Dante Gabriel Rossetti, young Hueffer (who later in his career used the name "Ford Madox Ford") had been brought up in artistic and literary circles in which everyone was expected to show creative talent. At twenty he had eloped with the daughter of a distinguished doctor, by whom he now had a little girl about the age of Borys. Bilingual in French and English, conversant with all the artistic theories of a generation, young Hueffer was at the moment getting close to nature by living in a rural cottage, where he was growing potatoes and lettuce on improved principles. He had recently moved out of Pent Farm in Kent, which was fairly comparable to the farmhouse rented by the Conrads in Essex. He proposed subletting the Pent to them, adding the attraction that it was partly furnished with his belongings, many of which would be priceless today for their connection with Rossetti and other artists of his school.

Conrad was all enthusiasm. Kent and Surrey were the

best counties for people who wanted the country but must live near London. Garnett, H. G. Wells, Henry James, and other acquaintances were not too far away for him to call. Hueffer's own cottage was no great distance off, which was especially convenient since Conrad had suggested that they collaborate on a novel. Stuck in *The Rescue* and unable for a considerable time to finish anything of novel length, he perhaps was doubtful of his power to do so. More importantly, he needed money and was conscious that he was too individual a writer to capture the market. If he were to strike the public fancy with a potboiler written in collaboration with a younger man, he would at least make his name known and could later write as he pleased.

During the next few years Conrad produced two novels in

Ford
Madox
Hueffer

collaboration with Hueffer which were neither good nor successful. The real effect of the partnership was that it provided him with the kind of companionship he needed. In those first years at the Pent, he was the possessor of an ancient "trap" or two-wheeled carriage with sides of basket-work originally painted a shiny black. In this equipage, drawn by a mare with ears so long that she looked like a mule, which he encouraged with loud cries and endearments in Polish, Conrad would constantly appear at Hueffer's cottage, to discuss a problem concerning their novel. Hueffer's own pony trap, slightly less disreputable, arrived equally often at the Pent, usually including Elsie and little Christina in the party. Both men worked late at night, but the cottage had no guest room, so that the Hueffers frequently moved into the Pent. Indeed in a certain sense they regarded the place as their own, since they were the original lessees and their furniture was still in it.

This arrangement certainly stimulated Conrad. He and Hueffer knew French literature at least as well as English and were both fascinated by every aspect of style, including the correct use of words, so that they would play a game together, searching for the best phrase to describe green wheat bent by the wind or a field of red cabbage. Hueffer had no great depth, but his surface sparkled. Emotionally, the two men were drawn closer by a common experience. Both were finding the support of a family somewhat of a struggle and had been taken slightly aback by the arrival of a child. Borys and Christina made demands which their fathers had not anticipated. "He can be naughty in more ways than you can imagine," Conrad wrote of his son.

Unfortunately Jessie Conrad, who seldom took dislikes, detested Hueffer, of whom Stephen Crane once remarked: "You must not be offended by Hueffer's manner. He patronizes Mr. James, he patronizes Mr. Conrad. Of course, he patronizes me, and he will patronize Almighty God when they meet, but God will get used to it, for Hueffer is all right." It stood to reason that Hueffer patronized Jessie, whose attempts to keep up with her husband's interests were unavailing. Henry James, then at the height of his reputation, sent Conrad a copy of *The Spoils of Poynton* with a flattering inscription. Conrad refers to it in a letter, adding: "My wife is this moment reading reverently James's book and trying to distinguish its head from its tail. Her reverence is not affected. It is a perfectly genuine sentiment inspired by me: but her interest is, I suspect, affected for the purpose of giving me pleasure. And she will read every line! 'Pon my word it's most touching..."

Conrad could afford to be touched, because he did really value Jessie's qualities, appreciated her cooking, felt soothed by her calmness, and was flattered by her devotion. Neither of the Hueffers shared his feelings. Elsie, who was an intelligent girl, was apt to palm little Christina off on her hostess while she listened to the men's conversation. Elsie was not at home in the kitchen, and Jessie soon felt she was being treated like a servant.

Jessie did not exactly protest, but she lost no chance of making her attitude felt. When Hueffer invited James to tea at the Conrads' without giving notice, Jessie retired to the kitchen to make things ready, only asking her husband to fasten the kitchen door open because it was hot. Hueffer shut the door, on the pretext that a view of the kitchen did not look well, whereupon Jessie took her overall off and refused to prepare the tea till the door was reopened. One night Hueffer did not find her curtains thick enough and draped a blanket over them to cut out the light. Then, feeling cold, he rummaged around and piled on the bed Conrad's formal frock coat and striped gray trousers, which were carefully preserved for London visits. They were discovered in a rumpled condition on the floor next morning, and Jessie, of course, showed them to Conrad, whose growing shabbiness must have given edge to his annoyance. Such pinpricks gave her a good deal of satisfaction, but they were not enough to cut off a friendship which filled a real need in Conrad's life.

One of the first results of the stimulus of Hueffer's company was "Heart of Darkness," a long-short story which is the most subtle and interesting of Conrad's works to date. In form it is another story told by Marlow and based on Conrad's own experiences in the Congo. Like a jewel, "Heart of Darkness" has many facets. From one view it is an exposure of Belgian methods in the Congo, which at least for a good part of the way sticks closely to Conrad's own experience. Typically, however, the adventure is related to a larger view of human affairs. Marlow tells the story one evening on Hope's yacht in the Thames estuary as darkness falls, reminding his audience that exploitation of one group by another is not new in history. They are anchored in the river, where ships go out to darkest Africa, and indeed to all over the world. Yet, as lately as Roman times, London's own river led, like the Congo, into a barbarous hinterland where the Romans went to make their profits. Soon darkness falls over London, while the ships that bear "civilization" to remote parts appear out of the dark, carrying darkness with them, different only in kind to the darkness they encounter.

These thoughts and feelings are merely part of the tale, for Conrad has a more personal story to tell, about a single man who went so far from civilization that its restraints no longer mattered to him. Exposed to the unfamiliar emotional and physical demands of the African wilderness, free to do exactly as he chose, Kurtz plunged into horrible orgies of which human sacrifice and cannibalism seem to have formed a part. These excesses taught him, and through him Marlow, what human nature was actually like. "The horror!" he gasped before he died. Marlow's own journey from Belgium to the Congo and thence up the river now takes on the aspect of a man's journey into his own inner depths. Marlow was saved from the other man's fate not by higher principles or a better disposition, but merely because he happened to be very busy, and the demands of work were in themselves a discipline. We perceive, too, that other white men on the Congo refrained from such excesses, if they did so, only because they had lesser, more timorous natures which did not dare to express themselves completely. Marlow felt that he had taken the lid off something horrible in the very depths of man which he could not explain when he returned to the world where basic instincts have been carefully smoothed over. Faced by a crisis, he even denied what he had seen, though he was appalled by his lie as bringing with it a betrayal of truth which was essentially a kind of death.

Stimulated by collaboration with Hueffer, Conrad's own writing continued to go well for some time. *Lord Jim,* starting as a short story based on a sensational incident he had heard about in 1880, began to expand into a considerable novel, important for its insight into moral dilemmas which were of enduring interest to Conrad himself. While it is hardly fair to say that he felt conscious guilt for having betrayed his father's ideals, his family had certainly tried to make him feel a traitor to Poland when he chose to go to sea. Naturally he was drawn to the themes of guilt and atonement and interested in the picture of a man who, rejecting what he had done, still had to live with it. Subtle as ever, he shows us Jim through the eyes of other people, not only of Marlow, but of a seaman who knew what a tricky thing courage is, of a successful man afraid of failure, of a woman in love with Jim, of a disillusioned romantic.

One of the subjects which Conrad liked to discuss with Hueffer was the technique of presenting personality through fiction. On first meeting a man in real life, we may discover little beyond the fact that he plays tennis and can occasionally give us a game. Soon we learn how bitterly he hates to lose, which leads us to discuss him with other people, who tell us how he is at war with his own family. We do not start our acquaintance at his childhood, follow his character through its development, and eventually attend his funeral. In *Lord Jim,* Marlow first meets Jim when he is on trial for a moment of involuntary failure. This leads him not only to examine Jim in his own mind or through the minds of other people, but to listen to why he will not live with his guilt. Our acquaintance with Jim deepens with Marlow's as he gets his second chance, becoming Lord Jim of the Berouw River, virtual ruler of people who are never going to hear about his past. But the deed, once done, remains in his life if not in theirs. By a misjudgment which is really no fault of his own, Jim is tricked into what looks like a second betrayal. Deserting the girl whom he loves, he atones by his death, preferring his honor to her need with a lack of hesitation which she cannot help regarding as purely selfish.

Interesting not only in itself, but for its narrative method, *Lord Jim,* and later works by Conrad, proved a new influence on the English novel which would affect Joyce, or Faulkner and other moderns far more directly than Galsworthy ever could, because *The Forsyte Saga,* though a masterpiece of its kind, stands at the end of a long tradition, rather than at the beginning. Perhaps the other quality about Conrad which has interested the moderns had also begun to make itself felt. This is his deep, but courageous, pessimism about human nature. He regards man as possessing unchanging qualities which are not going to be altered by human institutions. On the contrary, political or economic systems, being creations of man, will always be just as imperfect as the nature from which they have sprung. Free from nostalgia and interested in the past only insofar as it reproduces the same imperfections and confusion as the present, Conrad looks on human nature soberly, regarding as heroes only those who are too young, too limited by education, or too insensitive to understand their own natures.

Lord Jim was finished in the middle of 1900 at the end of a marathon session of twenty-one hours. Conrad was always in a hurry to finish, like a racehorse coming into the straight. Creation was such a tremendous pain and worry to him that he never seemed certain that he could finish till near the end. On this occasion he was in a hurry to have done because he had promised to spend a holiday with the Hueffers in Bruges in order to work on the current collaboration. They achieved very little because Borys caught dysentery and nearly died. Jessie, for once in her life, was grateful to Hueffer, who was far more help in such a crisis than Conrad, whose emotional upsets invariably brought on his gout.

Returning to England without much done, Conrad and Hueffer spent most of the rest of 1900 on their joint work, save that Conrad produced a simpler story which has always been a favorite with his readers. "Typhoon" is a long-short story featuring a steamship carrying Chinese coolies through a hurricane. The storm itself is a companion piece to that of *The Nigger of the Narcissus,* and just as exciting. Captain MacWhirr, who is the hero of the tale, well illustrates Conrad's feelings about the limitations of heroic men. He got the *Nan-Shan* into the hurricane in the first place because his imagination was too restricted to perceive the dangers of what he was doing. After he had done this, however, his simple, straightforward nature was equal not only to the actual hurricane, but to the bizarre situation on board which it created. The action, not recounted by Marlow, unfolds straightforwardly, raising no profound questions save that of the limitations of the man of action.

Still in a successful mood, Conrad went on to "Falk," a tale of the East, and thence to "Amy Foster," a beautifully written story which portrays in an indirect manner his own history. The hero, a stranger from Austrian Poland, is shipwrecked on the coast of Kent, sole survivor of an emigrant ship going to America. Bewildered, he goes from place to place seeking help but, ignorant of the language, is repulsed everywhere as a lunatic stranger. The first person who offers him a kindness is Amy Foster, a dim-witted girl whom he eventually marries. But Amy, who is simple enough to have seen him as a man in the beginning, is gradually frightened by the strangeness which he shows in little ways. She transfers her affection to their child, whom she tries to protect from his influence. When in a fever he appeals to her in her own tongue, she snatches the baby and runs away. Next morning the doctor finds him lying face down by a puddle outside his gate. He had only wanted water, and he dies less of exposure than of loneliness and despair. Conrad portrays many lonely characters, since his view of human nature includes the fact that everyone is in some sense alone. Never again did he speak so clearly, however, of the feelings of a young man coming to England, incomprehensible, foreign-looking, and almost penniless. Despite its fictional plot, "Amy Foster" has a personal quality which is comparable, in a very different way, to that of "Youth."

9

The Years of Aspiration

I<small>N</small> H<small>UEFFER'S</small> <small>MEMORY</small>, fact is usually confused with fiction, but even he sounds reliable when describing how Conrad dreamed up schemes for raising money. He managed, or Hueffer says he did, to charm his grocer into giving him three years' credit, an extraordinary tribute to the fascination of this foreign-looking man who still pronounced "these" and "those" as "thees-a" and "thos-a." Luckily his financial situation was somewhat eased by the suggestion of Garnett that he employ a literary agent. J. B. Pinker, who handled all Conrad's work after "Typhoon," was a believer in his worth who was soon induced to advance money in the hope of future royalties. It is pleasant to know that these loans were eventually paid back, but not until Conrad was a good many thousand pounds in debt to Pinker.

He was busy finishing "The End of the Tether" in 1902 when his kerosene lamp exploded and consumed the second

part, now lying ready and due at *Blackwood's* on the following day. Frantically he stayed up the next two nights, re-
writing while the whole was fresh in his mind. Thereafter,
he did his best to get what he could out of the insurance. An
agent, Hueffer says, came to look at the blistered table and
burned carpet, both of which had been owned by Ford
Madox Ford (the name Hueffer was using at the time of the
writing) and were now on their last legs.

"It looks a very old carpet," the agent said. "Almost time
the moths had it, isn't it?"

"But that's just what makes its value. My dear faller,
consider the feet that have walked on it."

"The table's very old, too."

"That's why it's so immensely valuable. Consider all the
people with great names who have sat around it. It's a historic table. That's what it is."

"I'm afraid we can't pay for historic associations."

"But that's just exactly what you *do* have to pay for. Consider what you would have to pay if Windsor Castle burned
down. Yet that's most incommodious as a residence. Dread-
fully old-fashioned."

The insurance company, we are glad to hear, reburnished
the table till it shone as never before, replaced the carpet,
and paid a substantial sum for historic associations.

Conrad was beginning to feel as though he had used up his
own adventures and must find something new to write about.
Presently he recalled a story he had heard off the coast of
South America when he was on the *Saint-Antoine* and had
discovered again in a book of memoirs picked up secondhand. It concerned a man who, in the turmoil of a South

American revolution, got away with a whole bargeload of silver. In his usual manner, he approached this incident with the idea of writing a short story, which he thought for some reason might be comparable to "Youth." Since, however, his short visit on the *Saint-Antoine* comprised his total experience of South America, he began to immerse himself in background reading.

It is truly said that a man can only write about what he knows, and in the case of Conrad this is particularly true. He himself complained that he had no inventive capacity; and when he did make up the plot, for instance, of "Amy Foster," he gave the heroine the name of his own maid and at least a little of the temperament of his wife. Conrad possessed, however, a great ability to enlarge his experience by reading. Lord Jim on the Berouw River is not just Jim Lingard, nor even the Rajah Laut himself. He undoubtedly owes something to Rajah Brooke of Sarawak, a fascinating Englishman who established himself as ruler of that island simply because he cared about the welfare of its inhabitants and had the ability to promote it.

When Conrad began to read about South America, he extended his experience in similar fashion. He had already borrowed for his hero that Corsican sailor of infinite resource, Dominic Cervoni. In fact, he had even got so far as to fix on the title of *Nostromo,* or "Our Man." But his love of realism led him to construct an imaginary country out of the flat plains and high sierras which he had seen, and then to people it with far more figures than were needed for the short story he had planned. *Nostromo* extended, and then extended again, as he began to include in it lessons he had

learned from the Spanish civil war, from the Russian government of Poland, even from the Congo. People who play
the game of tracing Conrad's stories back to their origins
have never had such a rich mine as *Nostromo* or come up
with more varying results. Other people are amazed at Conrad's power to create a whole country convincingly on the
basis of a couple of weeks off the coast and a few days ashore
some quarter of a century earlier. However performed, it
was a remarkable feat.

Conrad always agonized over his work, and *Nostromo* was
too complex to be tossed off easily. He was increasingly
troubled by gout, and, as he complained to Galsworthy, "My
dear fellow, it is not so much the frequency of these gout
attacks, but I feel so beastly in between, ill in body and mind.
It has never been so before." His condition was not improved by the failure of his bankers, which meant that he
had to return at once the money they had lent him. In
despair, he deserted *Nostromo* for a series of sea sketches
which he thought Pinker might place in magazines and
which eventually were published under the title of *A Mirror
of the Sea*. He tried his hand at drama, too, adapting a not-
too-successful short story called "Tomorrow" into a one-act
play. He did not really like the drama and had a great dis-
taste for actors, feeling that they got between the author and
his audience. A successful play, however, is a source of quick
money.

Jessie Conrad had made a success of her marriage, but not
without effort. There were occasions, for instance, when
Conrad was persuaded to leave her with reluctance and
bombarded her with anxious telegrams. At other times he

went off on business without letting her know. His nerves made him the most unpredictable of men, and his determination to work often made him turn on Jessie and tell her to get herself and the boy out of the house for the day and leave him in peace. He and Hueffer, working late at night, would raise their voices, stump about and, in the case of Hueffer, pound on the ceiling. It cannot have been easy to entertain a flow of guests at short notice, never to raise her voice or seem disturbed. Jessie, who was not an abnormally insensitive woman, vented her feelings, like many another excellent cook, by overeating. It was not too long before Conrad was joking that he always knew he had married quality but had not bargained for quantity as well. Jessie had had a bad knee since well before her marriage, and her increasing weight put a strain on it. Early in 1904, she suffered from palpitations, which caused Conrad to worry about her heart. He took her to London on a combined holiday and visit to the doctor, who was reassuring. Jessie went shopping; and as she came out of a department store, both knees gave way. She slipped on the pavement, very seriously damaging the weaker knee.

Neither Jessie nor Conrad knew at the time that Jessie was crippled for life, but the effect of her accident was soon apparent. Deprived of any chance for exercise, Jessie grew more enormous than ever, which in turn put a further strain on her injured knee. Meanwhile the domestic work which she had performed must be entrusted to servants. Even at their poorest, the Conrads had a maid. An old farmhouse like the Pent absolutely needed one, and it was cheaper to save on rent and get a girl than live without one. From now, however, they required two or three; and there were periods when Jessie had expensive operations, needed a nurse, or must be supported by two people in order to move from bed to couch. Small wonder that Conrad's own share of their holiday in London was to write some part of *The Mirror of the Sea* and more of *Nostromo.*

Nostromo had become Conrad's most ambitious novel to date, for "our man," who must originally have been designed as the hero, had been superseded in Conrad's mind by the silver itself. This in turn led him to consider what exploitation actually means and whether a silver mine developed by North American money for profit would be capable of bringing happiness to the society of those who worked it. Conrad's experience of political life led to the conclusion that society was an extension of human nature and was for that reason always imperfect. With a compassionate smile, he portrayed Charles Gould, the mine-owner, to whom the mine itself became more important than the human beings who served it, or Don José Avellanos, the idealist who could analyze the misgovernment of his country and yet imagine that its ills could be cured by a simple revolution. The situation which made the stealing of the silver possible was a civil war whose causes were far above the head of the man who profited by it. Nostromo was a working-class Gould whose corruption took a more personal form because his character was far simpler. Yet Mrs. Gould, one of the most perceptive characters in the story, was able to see how the silver ultimately had destroyed both.

Nostromo has been compared to *War and Peace,* because both deal with issues which transcend politics, though they work through individuals. It is, however, a poor comparison. The exuberant Russian, composing his national epic about the Napoleonic war, has little in common with the deeply pessimistic Pole, building an imaginary country in a continent he hardly knew. *Nostromo* is a shorter, sparer work, which discusses the failure of mankind to embody its ideal; whereas *War and Peace,* for all its concern with ultimate values, is built on a success. The truth is, there is nothing quite like *Nostromo* in range; and its admirers are in consequence a special class. Its difference from other men's work is accentuated by Conrad's method of storytelling, which is once more to move backward or forward in time, revealing incidents in an order that is intended to direct the mind to the values lying behind them. But in *Nostromo* Conrad lacks a single narrator, since the theme is too big for a single point of view. The result, as critics have fairly complained, is that he tells the story by directing a flashlight on incidents at random. To some extent this does help to destroy the time sequence, suggesting vividly that Costaguana is getting nowhere. We are not, however, convinced that the order in which events unroll is the best possible. This flaw and the novel's pessimism are the chief reasons why simpler stories of Conrad's are often preferred. We may fairly say, however, that never did he aim so high, and that some will always prefer the larger canvas to the delicate miniature.

To finish *Nostromo* took the better part of two years, during which there was hardly a day when Conrad was not wrestling with it. He himself says that when the novel was finished he found his wife "heartily glad to learn that the fuss was all over, and our small boy considerably grown during my absence." The figure of speech well expresses his absorption, but hardly does justice to the fact that he was an affectionate father. Working half the night, he not infrequently took catnaps during the day, from which he would wake up to play with Borys. They shared a common interest in cars, so that early in Borys's life a contraption with four wheels and a primitive steering arrangement was being pushed up the road by his father with the aid of the prop from Jessie's clothesline. At the top of the hill Conrad would turn it around and, with an "Off you go, Boy," send it spinning back.

The demands of his son were not the only calls upon his attention. Mrs. George had never lost her hostility to her outlandish son-in-law, but was persuaded to pay the Pent a visit during the writing of *Nostromo*. Unfortunately, in the small hours of one morning she needed to use the outhouse which was the toilet facility of the Pent. Conrad, still at work at his desk and mentally in the comparatively lawless land of Costaguana, heard movements outside, seized his rook rifle, and rushed out to protect his household from intruders. Mrs. George fled in terror and was said by the family to have made several circuits of the house before she had enough presence of mind to take refuge in the building for which she had been making in the first place. In her agitation, she forgot to bolt the door, which was promptly burst open by Conrad, gun at the ready, shouting, "Come out, you, — damn you!" From that time on, Mrs. George did not visit the Conrads.

Life at the Pent always had an unpredictable quality, which was encouraged by Conrad's early obsession with cars.

As soon as these objects were brought to his attention, he managed to hire a four-and-a-half horsepower contraption, rather like a four-wheeled sewing machine, complete with driver. Since it would climb practically no gradient, Conrad and the chauffeur had to jump overboard on every ascent to run alongside pushing vigorously. It also had no reverse, a decided inconvenience in rural lanes which were apt to end in a farm gate. Pretty soon this vehicle was abandoned in favor of a twelve-horsepower model, which, according to one witness, broke down eighteen times in eighteen miles and certainly did manage to knock down a drunken sailor in Chatham, which called on Conrad's authority to disperse a mob. Molly, the long-eared mare, might be adequate to the weekly shopping trips to Hythe, a matter of about six miles. Further expeditions, from this time forth, became an adventure.

Nostromo was finished in the fall of 1904, at which time Jessie was to have a serious operation on her knee. Conrad, whose reaction to the prolonged strain of this major novel was a return to the restlessness of his youth, was determined to take the family to Capri for a holiday. Why his fancy lit on a place which had scarcely a yard of level land for Jessie's crutches cannot be explained. Nor do we know who made the expedition financially possible.

Jessie endured the trip with her usual calmness, even when being loaded and unloaded from boats strapped to an upright chair with her leg held out in front of her, supporting it by Conrad's scarf tied round her ankle. Capri at the time was no tourist resort, and the Conrads boarded with a peasant family with whom they ate all their meals. The

Galsworthys were not too far off, and occasional meetings took place. Conrad complained that the climate was too enervating for work, but the relaxation undoubtedly was good for him. His general condition was improved by a piece of good news which came his way. At the instance of some of his friends, who pointed out his great distinction in the world of letters and his small popular appeal, he was given a Civil List award of five hundred pounds. It was a lifesaver, and yet it came too late. Deeply in debt, burdened by an invalid wife, and struggling with an illness which demanded freedom from anxiety, he could not get back on his feet.

He returned from Capri rather unwillingly to revise his one-act play for production. Its single performance was well received, and Bernard Shaw, who had three plays running simultaneously, was flattering. Conrad, however, saw that the techniques he would have to study would hold up the production of any five-act play. He had to publish continuously in order to live.

He did continue to work, but was still feeling the reaction from the effort of *Nostromo,* and perhaps the disappointment when reviewers criticized it as being above the heads of the public. In December he was seriously ill, and decided that the English winter was too much for him. The family went to Montpellier in France, where Borys, whose education was becoming rather scrappy, took fencing and riding lessons. Conrad wrote apologetically about the extravagance, protesting with justice that there had to be some attention paid to the boy. He was feeling more cheerful, however, because he had an idea for a new novel, *The Secret Agent.*

When they returned to England, Jessie was pregnant. Her second son, John, was born in August 1906, at the London house of the Galsworthys, which had been lent them for the occasion, and which provided two hitherto unknown amenities, electric light and telephone.

The Secret Agent is the story of a man named Verloc who is paid by the Russian Embassy to infiltrate anarchist organizations of Russian exiles in London. Suddenly he is told to arrange for some atrocity which will induce the British to expel these foreigners. It is suggested he blow up Greenwich Observatory. In desperation, Verloc uses as his instrument his wife's half-witted brother, who lives with them. The attempt fails, but the boy is killed. Winnie Verloc, who has married her husband solely in order to get a good home for her little brother, stabs Verloc with the carving knife and eventually commits suicide.

The Secret Agent may not be anybody's favorite novel, because none of the characters is attractive. Even Winnie is so limited that we never care for her, though the final melodrama arouses a pity that we had hardly expected to feel. The anarchists, the man at the Embassy, the two police officers, even Verloc are examined with the detachment of a scientist looking at germs under a microscope. Yet the book is extraordinarily well written, dominated by an ironic mood which at times approaches humor. Perhaps this unity of mood, however, is not quite sufficient to make up for a lack of intellectual concept uncharacteristic of the author of *Nostromo*. We are constantly discussing men's views, conditioned by their professions of anarchist, spy, or police. We analyze them, but see nothing beyond to unify them all.

Joseph Conrad, Jessie, Borys, and John in 1908

Quite understandably, *The Secret Agent* had no better treatment from the reviewers than *Nostromo*. It was widely said that Conrad was a man who wrote for the few and not for the many. Magazines cared less about him than before, and sales of his books were miserably poor. It was depressing and irritating at the same time. "Ah, my dear," he wrote to Galsworthy, "you don't know what an inspiration-killing anxiety it is to think: is it saleable?" Meanwhile, his second winter in Montpellier had become an appalling disaster. Borys came down with measles which turned into pneumonia and bronchitis, causing the doctor to fear his lungs were affected. After a period of agonizing doubt, the Conrads decided to move to Champel, the Swiss hydropathic establishment which had done Conrad so much good in the nineties.

Unfortunately, just as they made the move, the baby came down with whooping cough and nearly died. Borys got it, though in milder form, and then developed rheumatic fever. Jessie, hobbling on her bad leg from one room to the other, never showed a sign of dismay, either before the children, or to her husband, whose nervous temperament was not calmed by the need for keeping on with his work. Not till August were all well enough to return, and by that time Conrad's accumulated restlessness was tired of the Pent. They found a new house in Bedfordshire, but no sooner had they moved in than Conrad hated its bleak exposure and would not be happy.

Hueffer, who had in the course of these events become less intimate because Conrad had ceased to care about collaboration, was now starting to edit *The English Review,* a literary periodical into which he planned to breathe new life. The Conrads were taking a holiday from their unloved house by spending a month in Kent, where *The English Review* was naturally discussed. Conrad agreed to write his memoirs for it. In December, when the first number was due to go to press, Hueffer turned up at the Conrads' with several assistants at an hour or two's notice. Jessie's carefully hoarded provisions for the month were hastily consumed. Candles and lamps were lit all over the house, and only the baby and the maids got any sleep. Conrad was working on proofs in his study, Hueffer, for some reason, on the stairs. Frequently they had to visit each other for noisy discussions. Jessie, concealing her resentment as usual, circulated with tall glasses of hot tea spiced with sugar and lemon, while Borys and his dog got generally in the way.

Hueffer had acquaintances and ideas, but lacked business talents and was no more able to cope with Conrad than, for instance, Pinker. Presently, when an attack of gout prevented Conrad from delivering the scheduled number of his reminiscences, Hueffer dramatized the fact in the magazine by regretting that owing to the "serious illness" of Mr. Joseph Conrad, the next installment would be postponed. The annoyance of Conrad was increased because Hueffer, tired of the encumbrance of Elsie and Christina, was having an affair. Conrad, who had shouldered the much greater burden of Jessie, felt sympathy for Elsie rather than her husband. Finally, Hueffer's business management had been so poor that the *Review* was soon taken over by Hueffer's brother-in-law, whom Conrad detested. One way and another, he decided to contribute no more. Hueffer complained that he had been made a fool of and criticized what had been already produced. The dispute worked up into a quarrel, which Jessie of course was at no pains to smooth over. An estrangement sprang up which was never really healed between Conrad and Hueffer.

Restlessly the Conrads moved back to Kent, where they took half a house in Aldington. Conrad was ill, but greatly appreciated a visit from a certain Captain Marris, who lived in Penang and knew the Lingards. There had been a good deal of gossip in Malaysia concerning who could have written about the Berouw River, Almayer, or the Lingards. "Joseph Conrad" did not convey anything to the friends of "that fellow who was mate in the *Vidar* with Craig," who had been someone with a long Polish name. Marris stirred Conrad up to write another trilogy of eastern stories, one of which, "The Secret Sharer," takes its place among his greatest short stories. Once again it presents a man who has almost involuntarily committed a crime which has sent him forever apart from his fellows, contrasting him with a young and untried captain who, by the mere luck of the draw, is succeeding in his profession. The two men, the story suggests, are interchangeable. Their fates are briefly linked, while the action which sends one into exile confirms the other in confident command of his own ship.

During all this time Conrad was working on another major novel, which would eventually be entitled *Under Western Eyes.* It had progressed slowly, and his production for a period of almost two years had been sporadic. Thus in 1909, when Conrad asked Pinker for more money for "The Secret Sharer," that long-suffering man demanded the novel. In exasperation, Conrad poured out his troubles to Galsworthy. "Does he think I am the sort of man who wouldn't finish the story in a week if he could? Do you? Why? For what reason? Is it my habit to lie about drunk for days instead of working?" For two years, he complained, he had not seen a picture, listened to a note of music. He sat twelve hours at his desk, slept six, and worried the rest of the time. What could he do more? He even threatened to burn *Under Western Eyes,* but actually finished the book by a tremendous effort.

Under Western Eyes is the story of Razumov, a student at the University of St. Petersburg, whose ambition is to graduate well and make some name for himself. One day, however, he finds at his lodgings a student named Haldin, whom he knows a little, who has just assassinated one of the political tyrants of the Russian regime. Asked to sacrifice himself, in effect, for a cause which he does not believe in, Razumov betrays Haldin to the police. The act enmeshes him in the toils of the police himself, so that presently he is sent to Geneva to spy on the Russian anarchists there. They receive him eagerly because they think that he has done his best to save Haldin. Haldin's mother and sister, who are also living in Geneva, wish to know and thank Razumov, who gradually finds himself hopelessly in love with Natalie Haldin. At last he confesses, not only to her, but to the anarchist circle, who revenge themselves on him. Deaf and crippled, he returns to Russia to live in obscure poverty, while Natalie dedicates her life to the unfortunate.

Under Western Eyes handles once more the theme of guilt and atonement, this time in a fashion which challenges comparison with Dostoevski's *Crime and Punishment*. Conrad, it is interesting to find, loathed Dostoevski, undoubtedly in part because he was Russian, but also because his own resigned acceptance of human guilt has little in common with the emotional redemption which a Dostoevski character experiences. Conrad makes no suggestion that Razumov is any better because of the destruction which he has brought upon himself. He is merely living as he is, instead of living a lie.

Under Western Eyes is not only a story of crime and

punishment, however; it is also a bitter indictment of Russian autocracy, which dominates the book, destroying with complete impartiality the impractical Haldin, the well-meaning Razumov, and the various anarchists who have undertaken to fight it. Choosing for his narrator an elderly English language teacher in Geneva, Conrad is constantly able to stress the chasm which exists between a Russian, helpless victim of his government, and any inhabitant of western Europe.

The novel was finished, but Conrad's nerves had finally reached breaking point. He insisted on taking up the last pages to flourish them under Pinker's nose and, not surprisingly, had a furious quarrel with him. Returning home, he came down with gout which soon developed into a physical and nervous breakdown. He held long conversations with his characters, would neither touch his manuscript nor let anyone else work on the corrections. He accused his wife and doctor of conspiring to shut him up in a mental institution. After about three months he had more or less recovered, but he was undoubtedly shaken by the experience. He said that the nervous tension of the past few years had to result in such a breakdown, but he could not just dismiss it after it happened. Some change of which he himself was hardly conscious had taken place. He was unwilling to wrestle any longer with the great themes of guilt and atonement, of political and private realities. It was easier and safer to close certain doors in the mind.

10

The War Years

Under Western Eyes was received with appreciation of its brilliance, but its pessimistic tone and Russian setting prevented it from becoming popular. Yet, even while critics were repeating that Conrad was a novelist for the select few, the tide was actually beginning to turn in his favor. Perhaps the first sign was a government pension of a hundred pounds a year in recognition of his services to literature. Even more significant was an offer from Gordon Bennett, proprietor of the New York *Herald,* to serialize a new novel. Presently Conrad was hard at work on *Chance,* a story with which he had been tinkering for some time and which was finally completed in March 1912. For the first time, Conrad had written a best seller.

A great deal of his success was due to the *Herald,* but even more to the gradual build-up of Conrad's own reputation. By now he was well known at least by name as a master of English prose and a pioneer of new structures in the novel. In *Chance* these qualities could be enjoyed inside a love story which made no great intellectual demands on the reader. The book had a good title; Conrad had juggled the ending into a happy one for the sake of the *Herald;* and it took up topical subjects such as women's rights. Curiously enough, though Conrad's individual style was for the first time widely read and applauded, *Chance* is carelessly written. His right hand was becoming so crippled that most of *Chance* had to be dictated. The presence of a secretary fretted his nerves and may well account for a tendency to fill out long sentences with any odd phrase, to construct mixed metaphors, or to allow Marlow, the narrator, to wander off into generalizations which have not much to do with the story. The public, caring little about occasional faults, was overwhelmed by the merits which it now for the first time discovered.

Before he had even finished *Chance,* Conrad was feeling the soothing effect of a steady flow of money from Pinker, with whom he presently made up his quarrel. At last, that fame he had long sought lay in his grasp, bringing with it the agreeable flattery of intelligent admiration. A young man called Richard Curle, who had written an appreciation of *Nostromo,* was introduced to him and soon became anxious to write a book about his work. Hitherto, Conrad's friends had tended to be of his own standing, famous, if at all, in their own right. Curle, who could by age have been Conrad's son, developed into the great man's follower, appreciative and affectionate, but distinguished chiefly because he was intimate with the master.

Jessie Conrad, Borys, American author Ellen Glasgow, and
Joseph Conrad in 1914

Conrad's health was never good, but he was at least able
to go on from one creative effort to another. In June 1914,
he completed *Victory,* which to many people is his greatest
novel. Once more a love story is the main interest, together
with an analysis of a man who wanted to be a looker-on at
life. It is never clear why Heyst, naturally compassionate
and giving way to his feelings on at least two occasions
which other men might have passed by, should have been
permanently warped by the teaching of his father; but at all
events his predicament was one which Conrad understood
from experience and wrote about with feeling. The villains,
dredged though they actually were out of Conrad's retentive memory, remain cardboard characters, except for the
hotelkeeper, Schomberg. The situation, however, is developed in a beautifully logical sequence, which carries us from
one contrived suspense to another. If the story is not Conrad

at full stretch, it is certainly Conrad in perfect mastery of his technique. Nor could anyone imagine that *Victory* was a novel for the few, rather than for the many.

By 1914, the sales of *Chance* and the very substantial advances he received on *Victory* had put Conrad in a comfortable position. He could actually afford to take a holiday, and the moment seemed a good one. Borys, who had graduated from a nautical school aboard the H.M.S. *Worcester,* had been unable to take up a commission on account of his eyesight and was trying, without too much success, to get into Sheffield University. For the present he was at home, and might spare his family the summer. John, now nearly eight, was old enough to travel easily. Conrad had recently become friends with a Polish expatriate leader called Joseph Retinger, whose wife's parents lived near Cracow and invited both families to visit them. Conrad was greatly tempted. He had met criticism from time to time in Polish papers for donating, as it were, his genius to the English; but his increasing fame had swallowed complaints, and Poland was proud to welcome him on any terms. He was pleased with the notion of showing the scenes of his childhood to Jessie and the boys, who did not speak Polish or understand very much about his background.

It was an attractive scheme, waiting only for *Victory* to be revised and off his hands, which would not be until the end of July. Like other Europeans, he paid scant attention to the murder of Archduke Franz Ferdinand of Austria on June 28 by Serbian terrorists. It seems extraordinary that he, of all men, should have failed to understand the repercussions of a deed charged with the passion of Slav nationalism, or that Retinger, politically interested in eastern Europe, should have gone on making his plans for a visit to Austria.

On Friday, the 24th of July, the British Cabinet was interrupted in a crucial session on Irish affairs to listen to the text of an ultimatum sent to Serbia by Austria on the preceding day, in consequence of the murder of the Archduke. It was couched in language which one independent country did not customarily use to another and demanded terms which it seemed impossible that any government could accept. About this time, the bell rang in the Houses of Parliament to signify a division on some routine issue, and the Cabinet filed out to record its votes. As the ministers came into the House, a distinguished opposition leader asked Winston Churchill anxiously what decisions had been made on Ireland, which was on the brink of civil war.

"None of this matters now," Churchill told him. "In a week, all Europe will be at war."

The morning after this incident, the Conrads in high spirits embarked on a boat for Hamburg, en route to Austria, the very focus of the trouble.

On the 27th, they arrived in Cracow, where they were to spend a few days, while Tola, Retinger's wife, went ahead to see her family, some thirty miles distant. The Austrians, who had by now declared what they thought would be an easy war on Serbia, had mobilized only their southern districts in order to avoid provoking Russia, Serbia's ally. Russian and Austrian general staffs alike were urging their rulers that their country's military machine was not geared to mobilization in part or in one district. The general public, however, was not alarmed, relying on Germany to frighten Russia out of declaring war.

The Conrads got to their hotel in the early evening, in plenty of time for dinner, and were actually in the middle of eating when the entrance of a tall gray-haired man caused Conrad first to stare and then to bound up with a cry of recognition. The stranger, who was of course one of his old school friends, passed the evening with them and invited them to spend the following day at his country home a few miles outside Cracow. But even after this friend had left, Conrad was too excited to go to bed. He took Borys out to show him the Market Square and the towers of St. Mary's by moonlight, pointing out the Florian Gate and the site of his first school.

Next morning they set out for the country in a hired car, an elderly convertible which leaked, since it happened to be raining. The driver apologetically remarked that, as it probably would be requisitioned soon, it had not seemed worth fixing. Jessie, whose inability to read the papers had insulated her from the growing crisis, received a shock which she concealed under her usual placid manner. They were welcomed hospitably by their hosts and spent an enjoyable day until, as they were considering getting back to Cracow, their hostess burst into the room with news. A general mobilization order had been signed and a troop of cavalry were taking the horses out of the plows and commandeering every vehicle that would move. Conrad's argument with the officer in charge about the hired car was luckily resolved by the appearance of Jessie, walking painfully on two sticks. They were permitted to leave, passing a field where another officer was making a list of horses on a table he had requisitioned from a neighboring farmhouse. Presently the Conrads rescued an old lady, whose carriage stood horseless and abandoned on the highway, giving her a lift into Cracow, where their hotel proprietor met them with his hair already cropped in a military cut. He was off to the barracks.

Serious at last, the Conrads faced the growing crisis. Russia and Austria were mobilizing their forces, while Germany was threatening Russia with war. Since every country knew the other's mobilization timetable, no one of them could afford to be left behind. A group of Polish friends gathered in the hotel, all appalled by a war which divided the German and Austrian parts of Poland from the Russian. Joseph Retinger, whose wife was actually across the Russian frontier, determined to drive to the border and see if he could not bribe a peasant to send Tola a message. Conrad took Borys aside and asked him to go along in order to dissuade Retinger from crossing the border himself.

They set out once more in the hired car, but the Austrian officer in charge at the frontier told Retinger that he would be shot if he tried to go across. Since, however, the Russians had withdrawn twenty miles as part of a last-minute effort to avoid hostilities, two Austrian soldiers went across and captured a peasant, who was offered a large sum of money to take a message, half at once and half when he returned with Tola.

There was nothing to be done but wait all night. Borys played chess with one of the guards, while Retinger paced the floor. By dawn it was evident that the peasant had either gone home with the money or been captured by a Russian patrol. Tola was not coming.

Civilian trains would run, it was announced, for a couple more days, subject to delays for military traffic. Appalling scenes were being enacted everywhere, as people tried frantically to get home before war was declared. Retinger, member of an important Polish committee in London, felt it his duty to go, leaving Tola with her parents. Conrad, who was as usual in moments of crisis suffering from gout, hesitated to plunge his family into the confusion, which would probably leave them stranded in Germany. Jessie was badly crippled and might be injured by the milling crowds fighting for place on the last train, while John had chosen this moment to run a temperature. For a few days, therefore, they stayed where they were, while Conrad deliberately made contact with influential Polish people in case the Austrians should cause them trouble. He took Borys everywhere with him, visiting, among other places the University, where he was shown in the Jagellon Library papers and letters of his father's which he had thought were long since destroyed.

It soon became obvious that they could not stay where they were. Cracow was right in the path of a Russian advance, and in any case their rooms were requisitioned. Conrad had a cousin who ran a boardinghouse in Zakopane, a resort about four hours away by train, in the mountains, and therefore out of the path of the tornado. The family was traveling under Conrad's legal name of Korzeniowski, and he still imagined that the Austrians would not bother a Pole for the duration of a war which everyone supposed would be short. They started out for Zakopane in such a hurry that Jessie, who had been getting the family laundry done while decisions were being made, had to pack one trunk full of damp clothes and hope for the best. There was no staying, since already before they were out, soldiers had come up to take over their rooms.

Zakopane was crowded with refugees, in many cases parts of families. Tola Retinger had found her way there, too late to get home with her husband. One mother had lost her nurse with three of her children, two of whom died in the subsequent confusion. Trains full of travelers piled up at the station, so that pretty soon food began to run short in the district. Jessie spent all she could in buying supplies, but that trunk with the damp clothes had never arrived, with the consequence that the Conrads had John's favorite engine, their formal costumes, the minimum of underwear, and almost nothing heavy enough for the cool air of the mountains. They had to buy a few garments, but there were shortages, while outsizes for Jessie were hard to come by.

Conrad had written to Pinker for a hundred pounds, but could not be sure whether or when the letter would reach him. On August 1, France gave Germany to understand that she would support her alliance with Russia. The Germans, whose plans had been worked out years earlier, immediately attacked France through Belgium, thus bringing in England, who had guaranteed Belgian neutrality. By August 4, all Europe was ablaze, though England's position to Austria was not yet defined. From Zakopane, where telephone and telegraph had been cut off, Conrad wrote another letter, asking Pinker to send half the money in gold sovereigns, which might be exchanged more easily than British banknotes. Both his letters were returned marked UNDELIVERABLE BE-CAUSE OF WAR. By this time, however, Conrad was in touch with Polish friends in Cracow who were trying to get him a permit from the military commandant to travel to Vienna. Here he proposed to contact the American Ambassador, who might be expected to take a special interest in him because the head of his American publishing firm, Walter Page of Doubleday and Page, was American ambassador in London.

The military commandant duly sent a permit, scribbled on the back of one of his visiting cards, to allow the Conrads to return to Cracow, where arrangements would be made to send them to Vienna. There was no time to be lost; it was already the middle of October; and indeed it is a striking tribute to the last remnants of nineteenth-century civility that none of Conrad's requests to travel resulted in the internment of Borys, now seventeen and almost of military age. Luckily the Austrian bureaucracy, renowned for its old-fashioned slowness, had been thrown into so much confusion that it had not yet gathered in the aliens inside its borders. Jessie spent an evening packing, and the family started off in a snowstorm at midnight to drive in a clumsy open carriage to the railroad station which served Zakopane, about thirty miles away. After a long wait, they crowded into seats already occupied by four persons in heavy sheepskin coats and a large number of fleas. Jessie's leg was propped on the opposite seat, and she managed miraculously to produce sandwiches of canned chicken, tongue, and corned beef, together with cans of spaghetti and tomato which she actually heated on a spirit lamp. It took them eighteen hours to get to Cracow, where they found the station surrounded with barbed wire and jammed with soldiers. Fortunately their friends had been able to get them rooms at the hotel, while the commandant promised their travel permits should be ready in the morning. Friends warned that there was cholera among the troops, and one of them was able to produce four army-type water bottles which were carefully filled with boiled water. Jessie was busy arranging for the packing of more food.

Next day the Conrads went back to the railway station, where they sat for eleven hours, while long trains came in from the frontier carrying prisoners and wounded. The floor, soon slippery with blood, was occasionally covered with disinfectant and a few shovelsful of sawdust. The train to Vienna was full of sick and wounded, but luckily the commandant had sent an aide to help the Conrads, and a small compartment with two benches was soon cleared for them. It was, however, completely stripped; the cushions, presumably soaked with blood, had been ripped off, the glass cracked or removed. They spent over twenty-four hours on a journey which usually took five hours and a half, but their food and water luckily held out.

In Vienna they found a hotel, and Conrad, after reporting their arrival to the authorities and also to the American ambassador, Mr. Penfield, went to bed, ill and worn out. Not so Jessie. After a good night's sleep she announced her intention of searching for their lost luggage. Borys found her a cab driver who knew some French and English, with whose aid they made a round of storage depots, many of them piled to the roof with lost luggage, completely flattening such trunks as happened to be near the bottom. Invincibly obstinate, Jessie finally discovered her missing possessions and bribed the railway people to disinter them from an immense heap. She returned in triumph, but did not dare open the mildewed trunk of wet clothes until they could be washed.

Meanwhile, Mr. Penfield was using his influence and after some time actually produced a permit to travel to Italy. He was uncertain whether it would be honored, but it was important that the Conrads lose no time in getting away. Accordingly they left for the frontier, where they found the Austrian guards had been replaced by Germans in an effort to tighten up the regulations. Conrad, who always claimed that he only spoke a little German, became remarkably fluent on this occasion, but to no avail until he opened his British passport and pointed to the German visa. To his astonishment this did the trick, the guard evidently overlooking the fact that the actual passport shown to him was British. They made all haste to get over the border, while the bureaucracy in Vienna, ponderously going through its motions, produced in about two weeks an order forbidding the Conrads to leave the country until the end of the war.

The four years of war which followed this adventure hit Conrad hard. In his late fifties and of uncertain health, he fretted because he was of little use. The magnitude of the slaughter, the long-drawn-out agony of the Europe he had known took his attention from creative work. Borys, unenthusiastically tutoring for Sheffield University, preferred to enlist; and Conrad saw that he got a commission because of his background on H.M.S. *Worcester*. He was trained for the artillery and in a surprisingly short time sent to the western front. The arrival or nonarrival of news was naturally a fresh strain on Conrad and on Jessie, who concealed it beneath her usual manner.

In 1916, Conrad volunteered his services to the government, which was delighted to make use of his talents to publicize the work that the navy was doing. Accordingly he visited various ports, went out with a mine sweeper on patrol, and made a flight in the open cockpit of one of the primitive airplanes of those days, refusing to put on proper headgear for the purpose, but consenting to tie his derby on with the aid of his silk scarf. Finally he went out on a q-boat, a subchaser disguised as a merchant ship, which was the most hazardous duty the navy offered in those days. Pretty soon, however, his health gave way under the strain, and his job lapsed. He wrote an article or two and a short story, not one of his best. Since, however, he was well enough off not to need to write, the anxiety of the times prevented him from concentrating.

Typical of the restless unhappiness of those years was the meeting with Jane Anderson Taylor, an American war correspondent of outstanding beauty and charm who was using her natural talents in the pursuit of news. A chance meeting made her known to the Conrads, with whom she soon became intimate. In fact, she accompanied Jessie on a seaside holiday on one of the occasions when Conrad was absent on business for the navy.

It had been a long time since Conrad had spent so much of his life away from Jessie. All around him other families were breaking up in similar fashion, throwing him with professionals who were for the moment unattached. Responding to an atmosphere familiar through much of his life, he found himself strongly attracted to Jane Anderson, who had the social and intellectual charms of Marguerite Poradowska and provided the glamour which Jessie lacked. Yielding to temptation, he wrote a love letter to her.

Miss Anderson, who was actually married to an American reporter and who certainly had her pick of men younger than Conrad, may possibly have felt that things had gone too far. It is equally likely, however, that she was anxious to break up his marriage with what another intelligent woman was to call his "lump of a wife." At all events, she boasted to Jessie about her letter, precipitating a situation which Conrad had not bargained for. His devotion to Jessie, who represented home and roots in England, may not have been romantic, but it was deep. Faced with a choice, he had no hesitation in cutting off his acquaintance with Miss Anderson. It is a measure of his feeling for her, however, that he was angry when she entered into a liaison with Retinger, whose wife remained in Austria for the duration of the war. A coolness arose between the two friends which was never entirely overcome.

It may have been as a result of this entanglement that Conrad's thoughts went back to a woman whom he had loved when he was in Marseilles. He began a new novel in the form of a series of letters from an elderly man to the love of his youth, but soon decided on a more conventional form. He called his heroine Rita de Lastaola, intending to sketch her as a Cleopatra-like figure endowed with the fascinations of women of all time. The book, completed shortly before the end of the war and entitled *The Arrow of Gold,* was widely hailed as autobiography in fictional form. This view was encouraged by Conrad himself, who not only told his friends that the story of Rita was a true one, but admitted that there were "some of these . . . episodes of which I cannot think now without a slight tightness of the chest."

Unfortunately, the real story of Rita cannot have been literally told in *The Arrow of Gold.* According to the novel, she was the mistress of Don Carlos, pretender to the throne of Spain, who was at that moment fighting for his crown and for whom Conrad, under the alias of M. George, was smuggling arms. The syndicate which bought the *Tremolino* for this purpose was inspired, he says, by "Doña Rita," who had come to Marseilles to work for the Pretender, though she was frowned on in more conventional circles, such as those of the shipowner Delestang. With Rita, M. George had a love affair, which was broken up by a duel with Blunt, an expatriate American in the Pretender's service, who wanted to marry Rita for her money.

On examination, this account of Rita does not fit the facts any better than the duel or the tale of the *Tremolino* recounted in *A Mirror of the Sea.* Don Carlos did indeed have a mistress, called Paula de Somogyi, a Hungarian actress of peasant origin very similar to Rita, who did wear in her hair a jeweled golden arrow. By a glancing reference to an episode in Venice, Conrad clearly identifies Rita with Paula. At the time in question, however, Paula was only eighteen, spoke neither French nor Spanish, had not the experience to act as the Pretender's agent, and was almost certainly never in Marseilles. Nor was Don Carlos in Spain, for he had already given up the struggle. We may add that although the Pretender had not much character, what there was of it was royal. He had a strong sense of his own rights, which makes it hardly conceivable that he would have tolerated a liaison between his mistress and an obscure young man — about which jealous bystanders would have been quick to inform him. In other words, whatever Conrad may have said concerning the truth of his tale about Rita, he did not have literal truth in mind and was concealing, in his usual way, even more than he revealed.

Rita de Lastaola seems to be a composite figure, owing something to Paula de Somogyi, probably admired from a distance, something to Jane Anderson, Marguerite Poradowska, and even to earlier loves of a schoolboy in Poland. As an individual, she never comes alive in *The Arrow of Gold,* which is among the worst of Conrad's books. His invention of details in the plot, however, and his combination in one person of all the glamorous females he ever knew, cannot be considered proof that there was no Rita in his life at Marseilles. Perhaps the amount of money which we know Conrad wasted at this time may indicate an expensive affair with a Carlist lady whose identity will never be known. In *The Arrow of Gold,* the idyllic love affair between Rita and M. George is broken up when George goes into Marseilles to get more money and learns that Blunt is spreading false stories about him. He fights a duel and is wounded. Rita nurses him till he is out of danger and then silently goes out of his life, leaving behind her the assurance that he was her real love. This ending, many people felt, needed some explanation. Conrad, when asked why Rita had deserted her lover, replied that she would have ruined him. George was young, had a profession, needed to work and make something of his life. He could not become an appendage to a wealthy courtesan. This reasoning, though never set forth in the book, could have been behind Conrad's flight from Marseilles. The lady, as events proved, had done him no good; and he was content to let the affair lapse.

The literal truth about Rita de Lastaola will presumably never be known. We have to be content with the fact that Conrad regarded the episode as important to him. We may point out that Thaddeus evidently knew nothing about a love affair. We may argue that a man so shy that he cannot even discover that a lady is engaged before he proposes does not sound like a man who has already had an affair with a woman. We may even say that a man who lives intensely in his own imagination might translate an adolescent adoration into the story of a love affair and even feel that from his own point of view he was probing the depths of a relationship of which the lady had been literally unaware. Much depends on how we judge Conrad's personality, how deeply we think him affected by that flight from reality which brought him through his tragic childhood. Is he trying in *The Arrow of Gold* to express his dreams or a boy's actual experience with someone more mature? Conrad does not wish us to know and has preserved his secret. Perhaps all that we can confidently say is that in Marseilles he dreamed of love.

11

Postwar Years

BY THE MIDDLE OF 1918, Conrad had finished *The Arrow of Gold* and had turned back to *The Rescue,* that novel about Lingard, "the king of the sea," with which he had wrestled in vain nearly twenty years earlier. He was not much over sixty, but already had a feeling that he should make something of the idea before it was too late. The war had aged him, and Jessie's state of health was much on his mind. Early in the year, she had gone to another specialist, who had put her leg in a heavy metal brace to reduce the inflammation before she underwent another major operation. When this took place in September, Borys got ten days' leave to come over and see her. Returning to the western front only a few weeks before the end of the war, he was buried alive by the debris of exploding shells and dug out gassed and shell-shocked. Meanwhile, to Conrad, realist and European, the fourteen points of President Wilson had little to do with

the accumulated problems that would need to be solved
before constructing a durable peace. Retinger, pressing for
an independent Poland, was anxious for Conrad's public support, while he, feeling that his loyalty was due to England,
preferred to let her come to general conclusions about the
chaotic state of eastern Europe before he supported any
policy.

These accumulated strains were increased by the necessity
of moving out of their home, Capel House, since the owner
had recently died and his heir planned to live in it. It was
hard to find a new home at the end of a long war during
which all building had come to a standstill, especially as
Conrad felt no ties to any part of England outside Kent.
Most fortunately, six months' furnished rental presented
itself, though Jessie, who was soon facing yet another operation, was anxious to see the family permanently settled.

During the war, Conrad had got about in a secondhand
Model T Ford, which he drove himself, to the terror of his
friends. His gout made him unwilling to have anybody
sitting close who might be thrown against him, with the
result that he put his guests in the back and, in the course of
conversation, not only turned round to speak, but made ex-
pansive gestures, lifting both hands off the wheel to stress
a point. Since Jessie, in 1919, was unable to walk, house-
hunting devolved on Conrad who enjoyed it if he had a companion with whom to discuss his unpredictable tastes. Borys,
whose physical injuries had not been serious, was soon
transferred to a neurological hospital in London, where
treatment proved to be nonexistent and discipline scandal-
ously bad. He was able to be transferred home where,

Jessie Conrad

though attacks of panic continued, he was well enough to drive his father about. The Model T was exchanged for a more modern car which, some months later when demobilization threw men on the market, acquired a chauffeur.

Oswalds, the home which the Conrads eventually discovered, was far more impressive than any place they had rented hitherto. The dower house on a big estate, Oswalds was an eighteenth-century building, of considerable size, surrounded by elaborate gardens, both formal and informal, which were separated by brick walls and old clipped hedges. It actually provided a drawing room, as well as a study for Conrad, who had always done his writing in what served at other times as the family living room. To keep up such an establishment, several gardeners and maids were needed, as well as the chauffeur, Conrad's secretary, who lived in, and Jessie's nurse, as often as she needed one.

By this time, the Conrads were pleasantly rich, or they would have been if money had not slipped away through Conrad's fingers. Pinker collected Conrad's royalties, paid his income tax, rent, and other fixed expenses, put a regular monthly sum to his credit at the bank, and was supposed to invest the remainder. Since, however, Conrad was always demanding extra cash, there was never anything left for the investments. Conrad, who had a morbid fear of leaving Jessie penniless, would make tremendous New Year resolutions, adding up foreseeable expenses and coming to the conclusion that he could well afford to live as he was doing if he would only be a little careful. A week after drawing up a most excellent budget, he would respond to a cry of help from some old acquaintance, an appeal for Polish charities, or a letter from one of his cousins ruined by the Bolshevik revolution.

Incurably generous with money, Conrad did not spend it on his personal wants. The books which lined his study were old paperbacks or picked up secondhand. He kept no collection of his own first editions or magazine serializations and accumulated the minimum of personal possessions. Though he was always meticulously tidy, he bought few new clothes; wearing his old coats with patches on the elbows when in the country. The pleasure which he got out of money was in giving to other people. This love of giving reached out to embrace friends like Curle or Galsworthy who were not in need, but for whom he was constantly picking up gifts, just

to express the pleasure he felt after so many years of borrowing. Fame had brought him new friends, which meant that
though he did not care for dining out, his own house was
constantly full of visitors. Anxiously he went over everything beforehand in order to provide each individual with
his favorite menu, wine, or cigar, the perfect bedside book,
or a midnight snack if he came by the late train.

The foreign courtesies which had taken Jessie's breath
away at their first meeting still expressed an endearing delight in seeing his friends. Conrad's good talk and his flow
of anecdote were as matchless as ever; but there were periods, too, of heavy depression when he preferred to sit with
his intimates in silence. Despite his willingness to discuss
almost anything under the sun, he did not like to give his
thoughts away and would take opposite sides of an argument
on different occasions, preferring to conceal his real conclusions. He had, however, certain prejudices which it was
well to understand, because the irritation of nerves which
went with gout was often uncontrollable. It was dangerous
to introduce the names of Tolstoy and Dostoevski into a
literary discussion, not only because both of these authors
were Russian, but because their emotional mysticism was the
opposite of Conrad's own view of human nature. To him,
a deed once done, a sin committed, was a permanent part of
the whole man which he must live with and could not throw
off by the action of repentance, even if it led to forgiveness.

His nerves made him especially unpredictable to those who
did not know him. To one well-meaning lady who said she
was sure that Conrad, the interpreter of mankind, must be a
good "internationalist," the Polish side of Conrad made in-

stant answer that such subjects were not to be discussed at his table. On another occasion, when a couple of dull callers interrupted his work, he was so irritated by the way in which one of them kept drawing her gloves through her fingers that he jumped up, snatched them from her, slammed them into a drawer, and resumed his seat with a smile of polite interest in what she was saying. Even his friends were not exempt from explosions, for which he did not apologize, attempting to make up for them by extra sweetness of manner and trusting those who knew him well to understand that on occasions he could not help himself.

Many of his literary friends were younger than he, and it is notable that there was one blank area where a friendship might have been expected. Naturally he knew Bernard Shaw and his circle, but the two were not intimate. Even H. G. Wells had drifted away from Conrad when he turned from science fiction to political novels. There was certainly a personal side to this coolness toward Shaw. The two were incompatible, Conrad being so touchy and Shaw incapable of resisting a chance to sharpen his wit on everyone around him. In the early days of Conrad's literary life, Wells had brought Shaw to lunch on a disastrous occasion when Wells himself was feeling ill and demanded dry bread and quinine water, while Shaw, the vegetarian, would take nothing but cocoa and a dry cracker. Conrad, who prided himself on his hospitality and had, despite his eccentricities, no fads which he imposed on others, was offended. This unfortunate impression might have been overcome, had not Conrad and Shaw been almost as different in their views as Conrad and Dostoevski. Shaw was what he himself described as a "world-betterer," obsessed with the notion that a change in human institutions would in itself reform mankind. He was, in other words, a convinced socialist; whereas Conrad, by nature and upbringing a conservative, objected to socialism precisely on the grounds that it claimed to remake human nature. Being political, socialism to him was a product of human nature with all the imperfections and limitations of its origin. Nothing was to be expected from it but the usual political seesaw in which different groups at different times were up or down.

This attitude toward Shaw and politics set Conrad apart from the intellectual movements of England during his time and essentially defined him as an artist. It should not, however, suggest that he had nothing to say about human nature that was not negative. The human community in his view was held together by positive virtues which did not need to be profound, though their application to situations often required great subtlety. In other words, he was a simple believer in duty, work, consideration for the rights of others, and courage. The qualities he admired were those he had tested at sea. They were often to be found, as he notes, in unintellectual people and sometimes were destroyed in men who were too clever. What made Conrad a great writer was not primarily his intellectual powers but his artistic ones. He was always conscious of this, but since he also had profound thoughts to utter, they served to increase the sense of frustration under which he labored. Seldom has any successful writer been so worn down by his efforts.

Richard Curle, who spent a great deal of time with the Conrads, both at Capel House during the war and at Oswalds

after it, says that everything Conrad planned revolved around
Jessie and that his devotion and consideration were endless.
Curiously enough, Jessie, though boasting of their mutual
understanding, dwells mainly on his perverseness. If, for
instance, she asked him whether he had turned off the lights
downstairs — for the Conrads had at last electric light — he
would bound down in a fury and turn on every light in the
place. The fact was, that though considerate of servants, he
could never understand why a house did not run smoothly
without effort on his part. Perhaps, too, Jessie actually invited explosions by a manner so imperturbable that she saw
her eldest son off to war with no more visible emotion than
if he were going out for a country walk. Borys recalls one
occasion when Jessie, who was usually when mobile to be
found in the kitchen, was standing by the stove propped on
a crutch when her husband appeared, demanding a letter
which he had received that morning and was later discovered
in his dressing-gown pocket. When Jessie replied in un-
moved tones that she had not seen it since he had it in his
hand, he went out, slamming the four doors between the
kitchen and his study, one after the other, with a series of
shattering crashes. Jessie waiting, frying pan poised, for the
last reverberation, lowered it onto the stove and went on
with her cooking.

For some time after the war, the Conrads had a common
anxiety about Borys, untrained for anything in civilian life
and still unsure of himself after his breakdown. Eventually
he went into a small radio business with a friend in London,
investing his veterans' gratuity and some money provided
by Conrad. In some senses Conrad's relationship with his

boys had always been good. Children liked him because he entered into their games in a practical spirit. Garnett found him once sailing with his six-year-old son in a laundry basket on the lawn with a sheet fitted up on a pole, solemnly swinging over the helm to come about and steadying her course before the wind. He had never punished his own children, contenting himself with screwing his monocle in his eye, making a truly devilish face, and shaking his finger. Nevertheless, he was with his sudden bouts of irritation an unpredictable, at times a terrifying parent. To this he added an affectionate interest in everything his children did. The

Joseph Conrad and his son John

relationship must have been difficult for a young man who had been for four years independent and was recovering from a nervous breakdown. His move to London certainly helped Borys, but unluckily the radio business collapsed after a year or two, consuming the money which his father had invested.

In the middle of 1919, *The Rescue* was finally completed. Conrad, whose love of purple passages of description had moderated greatly since his earlier years, had drastically revised the first part, but had not altered his fundamental plot. Lingard had undertaken to restore to their kingdom the exiled Prince Hassim and his sister Immada. All preparations had been made and the expedition was actually under way when it encountered a private yacht which had by accident been grounded on the very spot where fighting was due to break loose. Lingard felt a duty to provide for the safety of his compatriots which increasingly interfered with fulfillment of his pledge to the royal exiles. This conflict of loyalties was heightened by an attraction between Lingard and the wife of the yacht's owner. Half willingly, half unintentionally, Lingard finally saved the yacht's crew at the price of the lives of Hassim and Immada, setting the yachtsmen free to go back to their own world, taking with them the lady whom he loved.

The Rescue is an exciting tale; but Lingard is cast in the role of a romantic hero, struggling against circumstances rather than impelled to make a choice because of his inner nature. As a handsome, bronzed adventurer, attracting a woman bored by sophisticated living, he is the merest stock figure. What is more remarkable is that he fails from lack of the very energy which has been claimed as his outstanding characteristic. A strange paralysis creeps over him which we do not associate with Conrad's early creations. His collapse gives Mrs. Travers an importance which her personality cannot sustain. Conrad's women nearly always represent some force with which his hero inwardly struggles. Such is the function of Aissa, temptress of Willems in *An Outcast of the Islands*, of Jewel, the darling of Lord Jim, and even of Natalie, whose innocent trust breaks down Razumov in *Under Western Eyes*. Mrs. Travers, conceived in the same way, cannot advance to the center of the stage as Lingard retreats from it. On the contrary, when he lets her go, she passively submits to separation.

This weakness, central to *The Rescue*, had been foreshadowed in *Chance*, where hero and heroine nearly destroy themselves out of sheer diffidence. It appears also in *Victory*, where Heyst cannot defend himself or give way to his love for Lena till too late. In *The Rescue*, however, it seems to be grafted onto two characters who are intended to be commanding and decisive. For this reason it is worth noticing as a sign of a real fatigue in Conrad, which is something more than a passing mood, and which will develop.

It was not merely fatigue, however, which made him turn back to *The Rescue*. He had stuck in it many years ago, presumably because the conventional character of Lingard and his romance with Mrs. Travers did not suit him. Yet the twists and turns of the plot, the vivid sketches of minor characters, the pathos of Immada and Hassim, and the dramatic final crisis are clearly the result of hundreds of those imaginary sessions with Arabs, Malays, and half-castes which he spoke of during the writing of *Almayer's Folly*. Conrad had constructed his dream world with infinite pains, and not unnaturally he wanted to embody it in a novel. The remarkable thing is that, even though at the expense of his major character, he succeeded in creating a book of considerable fascination.

Conrad finished *The Rescue* in 1919 and, being still in the midst of moving to Oswalds and of his anxieties over Borys and Jessie, was as usual exhausted and unwell. Instead of embarking on any sustained creative effort, he turned to dramatizing *The Secret Agent* and a short story called "Because of the Dollars." Neither was successful, but Conrad complained of being mentally tired and during the whole of 1920 did little but work on background reading for a novel of Napoleonic times which had long been a project of his. Fascinated by the adventures of his great-uncle Nicholas Bobrowski and also by the intellectual upheaval which Napoleon had represented in Europe, he was considering a story set in Italy and based on Napoleon's escape from Elba.

In general pursuit of Napoleonic background as well as for the sake of a warmer climate, Jessie and Conrad decided to spend a few months in Corsica in the beginning of 1921. Borys drove them as far as Rouen, showing them some of the battlefields with which he was familiar. Jessie thought it would have been good for him to come all the way and share their holiday, but Conrad insisted that he ought to work hard to establish his business and not spend idle months in Corsica. They had left John at school in England and were soon settled at the Grand Hotel in Ajaccio, where they were joined for a while by the Pinkers. Conrad, fretful with his ailments, liked neither the hotel nor the weather, which was cold and wet. He complained that the mountain roads with their hairpin bends got on his nerves. Perhaps, he said, he would have done some work if he had stayed at home. As it was, though his secretary came out to join him, he did very little writing. The new novel, which was to be called *Suspense*, concerned itself with intrigue and counter-intrigue in Italy, generated by the presence of Napoleon in exile on Elba, not far off. It is hard to say whether the holi-day did any real good, since the rest of 1921 passed away in desultory fashion. There was a great deal of entertaining at Oswalds and an intermittent struggle with *Suspense*, inter-rupted by further periods of bad health. In December, Con-rad turned aside from his uncompleted work to write a short story based on the escape of Admiral Villeneuve's squadron from Nelson's blockade of Toulon in 1805, an incident which looked like a temporary reverse for the British, but was to lead to their naval victory of Trafalgar some months later. As so often happened, his short story soon got out of hand and developed into a novel called *The Rover*, which was finished in the middle of 1922.

It would be difficult to read *The Rover* without being con-scious of an increase in Conrad's sadness and fatigue. The hero, Peyrol, is another incarnation of our old friend Dom-inic Cervoni, but a very different one from the young, self-confident and energetic Nostromo. Peyrol is Odysseus returned from his wanderings, an old sailor and adventurer who has come home to rest from the sea. He has settled in a farmhouse on the coast near Toulon, where he can look out over the bay and see the sails of Nelson's frigates, relaying news to their blockading ships over the horizon. Presently the farm is visited by a French officer named Réal, whose task is to plant some bogus dispatches convincingly on the British in order to mislead them about French plans. He wants to use a boat belonging to Peyrol in which he will pretend to elude the British frigates, but will actually allow himself to be captured. At the last moment, Peyrol takes his place and is killed; but the dispatches are duly captured by Nelson, who believes they are genuine.

Peyrol is a fine figure, but unfortunately Conrad's splendid powers of creation failed him in dealing with lesser characters in the story. Arlette, the owner of the farm, is a beautiful young girl who was caught with her royalist parents in Toulon at the time of the revolutionary massacres there. After seeing her mother and father cut down before her eyes, she was seized by one of the revolutionists and forced to take part in the orgy of massacre until she hysterically yelled with the rest, part horrified, but part excited. Returning to her home before the opening of the novel, she was accompanied by the revolutionary Scevola, who passed in the district for her husband. Shattered by what she had been through, Arlette neither spoke nor seemed to recognize anyone — a state which continued for the better part of ten years. At this point, she fell in love with Lieutenant Réal; and we now learn that not only is she not married to the horrible Scevola, but that he, in whose power she has lived all this while, has never made love to her, even though he adores her and is jealous of Réal. Arlette trips off to the priest and, after telling him her story, becomes perfectly normal and can settle down to married life with Réal.

Conrad has the effrontery to portray the pair years later talking about Peyrol, whose sacrifice has made it possible for them to live happily ever after.

It is often the task of a novelist to make strange situations seem believable, but even Conrad's powers are not equal to this insult to common sense. It is true that with some of his usual subtlety he suggests a symbolic meaning for his characters. Scevola personifies the excesses of revolutionary France, Réal the discispline of the Napoleonic era. Arlette is the soul of France, prize of first one and then the other. These deeper meanings, however, cannot obscure the fact that the conflict between actual people on a farm outside Toulon is not convincing.

There is some splendid writing in *The Rover*, and Peyrol himself is an impressive figure; but it is the novel of a tired man. Conrad's careless treatment of Arlette is not the only example of failure to grapple. Peyrol has come home with a money belt full of gold about which he is secretive, and which appears to be going to play an important part in the story. Soon, however, it is forgotten and, after Peyrol's death, turns up in the well to enrich Réal and Arlette. Then, too, the whole atmosphere of the novel is tired. It is quite natural that old Peyrol should spend a good deal of his time looking out to sea in a haze of nostalgia. It is less probable that Lieutenant Réal should be almost equally lethargic, ready to spend long hours brooding together with Peyrol, vaguely suspicious that the inhabitants of the farm are signaling to the British and yet apparently unable to take action. The whole impression of the book is that of a man who longs for rest and is done with adventure.

12

Sleep after Toil

F. N. DOUBLEDAY, Conrad's American publisher, had
long been pressing him to come to New York. Conrad, who
was self-conscious about his foreign accent and consequently
did not like speaking in public, had many reservations about
a visit whose object clearly was to show him off. For one
thing, his health was unlikely to endure the strain of public
appearances. The Doubledays, however, were so understanding of his hesitations that gradually their plan began to seem
attractive. Finally he agreed to pay them a private visit,
spending the spring of 1923 on their Long Island estate.
Jessie, moving only with great difficulty, was to remain at
Oswalds, making a home for John in his school holidays
and keeping in touch with Borys, who had found a job with
the Daimler Company and was now in Manchester.

From the first, this was clearly going to be a tremendous
expedition, involving a positive trousseau of six new suits

with endless shirts and shoes and evening dress ties to match. Jessie came up to London with her husband for a couple of days, to see him off on the train for Glasgow, whence he was to sail on the *Tuscania*, whose captain was a friend. John was given leave from school to say goodbye, while newspaper men, alerted to the voyage of one of England's greatest living authors, arrived in droves at the hotel where they were staying. Amid the confusion, Conrad kept looking around for Borys and was distinctly hurt by his sending last-minute excuses about pressure of work. Not unnaturally, when a registered letter from someone unknown found its way into his hands, he passed it on to Jessie, too preoccupied with his own affairs to cope with extra problems. Opening it when she had leisure, Jessie was appalled to read an announcement signed by his mother-in-law that Borys had been secretly married in London eight months earlier.

There was no objection to the girl, whom the Conrads had already met; but at the time of his marriage Borys had lost his own and his father's money and was, or was shortly to be, out of a job. He knew that Conrad, whose own marriage had come late, would have opposed any wedding, and that it would have taken time and pressure to bring him around. Nervously affected by his war experiences and insecure in his relation to a father who still spoke and thought of him as "Boy," Borys had taken matters into his own hands. In Manchester, he was earning enough to support a wife, though perhaps not a family. His prospects, however, must have been far from certain in the confusion of postwar England. Naturally the longer he put off the revelation, the more difficult it had become. It was for this reason that he had not come to see his father off; but on hearing from Jessie, he volunteered to go up to Glasgow and break the news before Conrad sailed. Jessie immediately forbade him to do any such thing, convinced that Conrad would either cancel his American trip or fret himself to death while he was away. At the same time, he was bound to feel a certain disloyalty in Jessie if she accepted the marriage two months before he even heard of it. Accordingly, she refused to meet Borys's wife until Conrad returned, while Borys, on his dignity as a new husband, responded by breaking off relations until his wife should be acknowledged.

Innocent of this trouble at home, Conrad was soon basking in the warmth of a magnificent welcome. He was mobbed on the New York pier by forty cameras and more reporters than he had ever encountered, while a Polish deputation, including, he noted, some pretty women, rushed up with several enormous bouquets which they all wanted to hand to him at once. The Doubledays, though most considerate, had arranged a series of lunches and dinners for him to meet interesting people, including the Polish pianist Paderewski. Invitations to lecture, fan mail, and appeals for cash poured in from every side. Determined to keep his visit as private as possible, Conrad consented only to give one talk and a reading from *Victory* to about two hundred of New York's social elite in a private drawing room. This was received with such enthusiasm that, despite his inner nervousness, he was able to describe it to Jessie as a great experience. The Doubledays eventually rescued him from New York by taking him on a motor tour of Boston and New England. In June he returned to Europe, while his kindly hosts took passage on the same boat, apparently for the sole purpose of looking after him throughout the voyage.

Again he was hurt to find that Borys had not come to greet him on landing, and his reaction to Jessie's news of the marriage was violent. "I don't want to know any more about it. It is done, and I have been treated like a blamed fool, damn!" To the Doubledays, who politely hoped the young couple would be happy, he replied, "Well, they won't then. What's he got to keep a wife on? And let me tell you, I don't like the way this has been done in secret. I wasn't to know then, why should I now?" Poor Jessie, who felt she was blamed for keeping the secret, was hard put to it to maintain her placid air, as he announced to all and sundry, "My son Borys is married, you know. My wife knows all about it," interrupting any questions on the subject with an abrupt, "Damn!"

All the good of the trip seemed to be lost, and Conrad retired to bed as usual with gout. A few days later, however, he was arranging to give Borys an allowance, saying that though he did not want to meet his wife, he wished to avoid any sort of break. Needless to say, it was not long before the young couple were invited to Oswalds, though Conrad left Jessie to cope and took refuge in his study. Presently relationships were quite re-established by the arrival of a grandson; yet, whether because of the emotion generated by this episode, because the New York trip had been too much, or simply because his health was declining, Conrad seemed to have lost interest in things. His vitality was failing, and he could not settle down to writing. In July he made an effort to tackle *Suspense* once more, but it was evidently beyond him. In his weariness he had lifted the plot for this novel from the nineteenth-century memoirs of the Comtesse de Boigne, while his own hero, Cosmo Latham, a young man in his early twenties with nothing to do but travel for pleasure, is always feeling tired and remains essentially passive in a series of situations which happen to him. *Suspense* was planned on a grand scale, but Conrad's energies were no longer equal to another *Nostromo*. Despite some fine writing about the political situation and despite the appearance of the indomitable Dominic Cervoni in the guise of a smuggler carrying messages to and from Napoleon in Elba, the plot developed as slowly as the hero moved. Perhaps relying on a chance to revise which was not granted him, Conrad had even embedded in it pieces of the Comtesse de Boigne's work with the wording almost unchanged.

Conrad's writing life was coming to a slow end, but, before it did so, an event took place in New York which underlined the reputation which he had achieved in the world of letters. During the years of his poverty, Jessie had made useful money out of selling her husband's manuscripts, which she had carefully preserved, to John Quinn, an American collector. Conrad had received a couple of thousand pounds in all, most of it at a time when he was not widely known and needed cash. Thus he had nothing to complain of, though it was in fact a slight shock, when Quinn put the whole up for auction and disposed of it for the equivalent of over ten times what he had given. In the light of 1923 prices, $8100 for the manuscripts of *Victory* or $300 for four pages on "My Best Story and Why I Think So" were phenomenal indeed. "Did any of the bidders faint?" Conrad wrote to Doubleday.

"Did the auctioneer's head swell visibly? Did Quinn enjoy his triumph lying low like Brer Rabbit, or did he enjoy his glory in public and give graciously his hand to kiss to the multitude of inferior collectors who never, never, never dreamed of such a coup?" Whatever Quinn had done, Conrad was conscious that the sale itself and the excitement in the papers had put the coping stone on his reputation. ". . . thousands . . . who could not have read through a page of mine without falling into convulsions, are proclaiming me a very great author," he noted.

Success had come slowly, but it had at least come in full measure. The Prime Minister, Ramsay MacDonald, offered Conrad a knighthood; but he thought it inappropriate for an artist and refused it, as Galsworthy also had done a few years earlier. To universities which wanted to give him honorary degrees, he responded that his achievement was literary and not academic. Epstein, the sculptor, asked to make a bust of him, which Conrad liked, perhaps because it seems to portray him as the old seafarer, rather than the tired artist. "I am finished," he said during one of the sittings; but nevertheless he pulled out a drawer to show the manuscript on which he was still working, refusing to admit in so many words that he could no longer cope with it. It was four years, he remarked to somebody else, since he had written anything worth doing. All his writing life he had wrestled with the agony of creation, writing to all his friends letters which, as one complained, appeared to be written from the bottom of a pit. Then, however, his despair had been active, even furious. Now it was resigned.

In June 1924, Jessie's knee needed another operation, from

which she came home late in July to be for a time confined
entirely to bed. Conrad did not look well; and a few days
after she was installed at Oswalds, he complained of a sudden
violent pain in his chest, which might have been, he thought,
a heart attack. For a few days he took things easy and was
in bed early on the evening of August 1 when Richard Curle
arrived to spend a long weekend. Curle found him in good
spirits because Jessie was home again and he had discovered
a new house some eight miles off. After five years at Oswalds, he had been getting restless; but he did not want to
move outside the small area of England which had finally
become home. The new place would have to have electricity
installed, but he thought it would suit them. Next morning,
still cheerful though admitting to a bad night, he set out with
Curle to show him the house. Hardly had they got halfway
there before he again had a seizure of pain in the chest, was
induced to turn back, and was helped upstairs to bed. Soon
he began to suffer from terrible difficulty in breathing, com-
plaining of pain first in one part of the body, then another.
The doctor arrived in the course of the afternoon to find him
better and diagnosed acute indigestion. Hardly had he left
before pain and shortness of breath began again.

That evening, which was a Saturday, Borys, his family, and
John all arrived to spend the weekend by pre-arrangement.
Conrad insisted on having his grandson brought up to see
him, but his breathing was now so difficult that another
doctor, his own being unobtainable, was hastily summoned.
Once more when he arrived Conrad was better, so that the
second doctor, though he ordered cylinders of oxygen to
help the breathing, made the same diagnosis as the first,

namely indigestion which had induced asthma. Conrad himself, in one of his attacks, panted out that he was dying; but the family had seen him ill so often that no one was desperately alarmed. Rather, they were distressed by how much he suffered. "Go away, dear boys," he said to John and Curle, who were sitting with him. "I can't bear you to see me like this."

After a while he moved from bed to his chair and passed the night in this fashion, occasionally dozing. By morning he seemed easier so that around eight o'clock when Jessie in the room next door inquired about him, he was able to call out, "You, Jess, I'm better this morning. I can always get a rise out of you!"

He looked exhausted, but his pulse was normal. There seemed no reason why his manservant, who had been up with him all night, should not leave on an errand. Thus he was alone and Jessie, lying powerless next door, was also unattended when she heard him cry, "Here . . ." choke over the next word, and fall heavily. She called out in alarm, and people ran in to find him lying dead on the floor in front of his chair. He was not quite sixty-seven, worn out by the intensity with which he had grappled with three lives.

Joseph Conrad was buried in a corner of what he had made his own country, in the Roman Catholic cemetery of Canterbury in Kent. On his tombstone were engraved two lines from the poet Edmund Spenser which he himself had written under the title of *The Rover*:

> *Sleep after toyle, port after stormie seas,*
> *Ease after warre, death after life does greatly please.*

Above this, they wrote his name as Joseph Teador Conrad Korzeniowski, which, if not quite accurate either in Polish or English, did well enough for a man who, born in Poland and dying in England, had become to all who knew him simply "Conrad."

Conrad left behind him a body of work which has kept its popularity in the fifty years or so which have passed since his death. This is owing in part to the fact that his tales are about strange adventures, full of the physical demands which the sea makes on human beings. Many a hack writer has treated of such subjects and been forgotten. Conrad illuminates them by a style which, though highly elaborate and on occasions imperfect, does do what he desired, in that it makes the reader feel and see. In the second place, he has always meditated deeply on the experiences he has related. He is interested in the effect of a supreme challenge on the human being who either is equal to it or is not. He is writing, therefore, not merely about adventures, but about people, and particularly how they react to failure. His view of human nature being realistic, he is neither contemptuous of the man who fails nor overjoyed if he redeems himself. To him a human being is the sum of all his actions and desires and cannot cancel out one by doing another.

Since he writes about people, he writes also about communities. The *Narcissus,* for instance, is a ship whose crew comes together by chance, just as people are born haphazardly into one community or another. The *Narcissus* is a simple community compared to a world or a country, and its ultimate purpose is a simple one — survival. The virtues which keep it together are loyalty, courage, and willingness to accept the discipline of work for the sake of all. But because the *Narcissus* simplifies the issues of man in the community, it does not follow that what it says about the relation of social virtues to character, superstition, boredom, emergency, and the like contains no subtlety. Thus, if the first thing to say about a story of Conrad's is that it is highly readable and vivid, the second thing is that it has always something to say about life or human nature.

The third great quality about Conrad is that he is supremely an artist, not merely in words, but in the construction of a story. He can, as in "Heart of Darkness," write a story which appears to go on at several levels, each with its own meaning. He can, as in *Lord Jim*, interrupt time-sequence at will in order to make clear that, even while he recounts an adventure, his primary interest is in Jim's character, not because Jim learns to understand himself, or even because any one person ever understands him, but because he can only be judged by different people, each in the way in which his experience fits him to understand. Conrad can set his stories in a framework, sometimes to give them a sense of being a rounded whole in themselves, sometimes to suggest from the beginning that a tale has more than one meaning, and that each of these meanings has more than one level. Thus he is a novelist for the straightforward and the complex alike, vivid and engrossing to either.

These qualities have given Conrad a popularity which seems likely to be enduring. Yet, in an important sense, he is not everybody's novelist. There is a quality visible in his most ambitious works which is not precisely to everybody's taste; and it is no accident that while he was writing them, reviewers insisted that he was a novelist for the few and not for the many. Not everybody compares *Nostromo* to the mighty sweep of *War and Peace*. In libraries where "Typhoon" or *Lord Jim* are perennially popular, *The Secret Agent* and *Under Western Eyes* may be left on the shelf. Yet these are not worse written than *Victory* or *The Nigger*

of the Narcissus. Actually there is more in them to bite on. But who cares about Winnie Verloc, her tiresome half-wit brother, a few anarchists each more unpleasant than the last, and two policemen? Who cares about Verloc himself with his dirty little shop and his dirty profession and the lack of anything in his life which might ennoble it? Is it worth savoring such a novel, merely because it is perceptive about the way in which people are conditioned by their social situations?

Nostromo is a more likable book than *The Secret Agent,* but are we capable of creating a whole country with Conrad's help, a country so hopelessly misgoverned and going nowhere? Do we feel the sheer pleasure of analyzing causes of corruption? Can we take the trouble to follow the intricacies of a plot which is deliberately obscured by Conrad's method of jumping about in time? Are we rewarded for our efforts by realizing that Costaguana's government will not be improved? When the plot tails off at the end, as it does, do we feel that the grandeur of the whole conception sustains us? *Under Western Eyes* portrays the atmosphere of Russia under the Tsars — a vanished age. We perceive some likenesses, no doubt, to Soviet Russia; but the opposition with which the book is largely concerned bears no relation to anti-Soviet forces that we know about. It is hard to respond, therefore, to Conrad's theme that tyranny destroys those who resist as surely as those who submit.

The quality which makes all of these books difficult reading is a clear-headed pessimism about human affairs, a realistic acceptance of the fact that man has a very mixed nature which is not going to change, while human institutions will always partake of the imperfections of their makers. Without compassion, Conrad portrays the fate of Razumov, whose treachery has had some justification and whose confession reduces him to a life of misery. Never once does he suggest that Razumov is a better or happier man for having confessed. He is merely less torn because his nature has not been able to bear the situation into which his own original act had thrust him. The villain of the tale, the Russian Empire, goes on its way unaffected by Razumov's fate or that of any of the other characters.

We may leave such books on the shelf and still enjoy Conrad as one of the great writers of his age, a man who brought new vitality to the English novel, an author whose fascination can still be felt. If we do so, however, we have missed the intelligent skepticism of Conrad, which was one of his inheritances from his Polish past and one, incidentally, of his most modern qualities. We have not seen him rise above our natural likings in order to create an atmosphere where things at which we hesitate to look can be presented.

The great majority of those who admire Conrad will pass such qualities by, finding in his richness enough to attract them. Nevertheless, there are rare people who appreciate the difficult things that he wrote as well as the easy. For such readers, one might have inscribed on his tomb a different verse from Edmund Spenser's, as follows:

It is an ancient mariner,
And he stoppeth one of three.

It was never quite clear why the wedding guest who heard the story of the ancient mariner became sadder and wiser. But this revelation is granted to those who understand Conrad.

RECOMMENDED READING

CONRAD published both short stories and novels. Since, however, several of his novels are quite short and several of his short stories are quite long, there is little difference in some cases. For convenience, short stories may be classified as those which appeared originally in a book with other stories. In this case, the title of the whole book will be given in parentheses, though nowadays many of these works will appear in anthologies of Conrad, rather than in the original collection. The list which follows is intended as an introduction to Conrad and therefore includes only such works as have been most widely popular. For those who wish to read further, *Nostromo* is highly recommended.

The Nigger of the Narcissus	1898
Lord Jim	1900
Youth (Youth)	1902
Heart of Darkness (Youth)	1902
The End of the Tether (Youth)	1902
Typhoon (Typhoon and Other Stories)	1903
Amy Foster (Typhoon and Other Stories)	1903
The Mirror of the Sea . . . essays	1906
The Secret Sharer ('Twixt Land and Sea)	1912
Freya of the Seven Isles ('Twixt Land and Sea)	1912
Victory	1915
The Shadow Line (A Set of Six)	1917
The Warrior's Soul (Tales of Hearsay)	1925

INDEX

Adowa, the, 133–134

Africa, 111–114

AISSA (*An Outcast of the Islands*), 140, 205

Alaska, the, 73

Almayer, Charles, 95, 109; compared to Apollo Korzeniowski, 96; influence of, on Conrad, 96

ALMAYER, KASPAR (*Almayer's Folly*), 134; *An Outcast of the Islands,* 140

Almayer's Folly: compared to *An Outcast of the Islands,* 140; frequent criticisms of, 136; Jacques's opinion of, 130; publication of, 135–136, 138, 142; reviews of, 138–139; writing of, 109–110, 111, 117, 118, 124, 128, 134

"Amy Foster," 160

Annie Frost, the, 74

ARLETTE (*The Rover*), 208, 209

Arrow of Gold, The, 192–195; explanation of Conrad's wound, 56, 61

Bangkok, 98, 99, 100

Barr, Moering and Company, 84, 89–90, 109

Barron, Joseph, 87. See also *The Nigger of the Narcissus*

"Because of the Dollars," 206

Because of the Money (Apollo Korzeniowski), 11, 18

Belgium, 116, 117, 118; setting for "Heart of Darkness," 156

Berouw River, 93–94, 97, 109–111; setting for *Lord Jim,* 158; setting for *An Outcast of the Islands,* 140

"Black Mate, The," 90

Blackwood's, 147, 162

Blunt, 59, 61; *The Arrow of Gold,* 192

Bobrowska, Josefina (cousin), 27, 32

Bobrowska, Mme (maternal grandmother), 12, 14, 15–17, 21, 28, 30, 38

Bobrowska, Teofila (maternal aunt), 8, 15

Bobrowski, Joseph (maternal grandfather), 8, 14–15

Bobrowski, Nicholas (maternal great-uncle), 5–6, 7, 8, 206

Bobrowski, Stanilas (maternal uncle), 15, 22

Bobrowski, Thaddeus (maternal uncle): courtship of Conrad's parents, 8, 15, 16, 27–28; philosophy, 19, 34–35; Conrad's education, 32–35; sends Conrad to sea, 37–38; financial support, 38, 47, 63, 74–75; Marseilles correspondence, 51–52, 63, 64; the mythical voyage of the *Saint-Antoine,* 53–54; supports the duel theory, 54, 56, 57, 61; English correspondence, 68–69, 71, 74–75, 77–78, 128; visits Conrad, 83; Conrad's love for, 84; in ill health, 108; encourages literary career, 110; introduces Marguerite Poradowska, 116; receives a visit from Conrad, 116–117; Congo correspondence, 122, 127; final illness, 133; death, 134; legacy, 139

Bonnard, M., 54